S0-ABO-585

HOW TO GET RICH
IN REAL ESTATE

Other Books by Robert W. Kent

PRACTICAL REAL ESTATE BROKERAGE

(*in collaboration with Donald Corb*)

HOW TO GET RICH
IN REAL ESTATE

by
Robert Warren Kent

PRENTICE-HALL, INC.
Englewood Cliffs, N.J.

© 1961, BY

PRENTICE-HALL, INC.

ENGLEWOOD CLIFFS, N.J.

ALL RIGHTS RESERVED. NO PART OF THIS BOOK
MAY BE REPRODUCED IN ANY FORM, BY MIMEO-
GRAPH OR ANY OTHER MEANS, WITHOUT PER-
MISSION IN WRITING FROM THE PUBLISHERS.

LIBRARY OF CONGRESS
CATALOG CARD No.: 61-10321

Ninteenth Printing . . . . . June, 1977

PRINTED IN THE UNITED STATES OF AMERICA

40943—BC

To the SPARK in some men that makes them say, "I will NOT accept the fate handed to me by the accident of life. I will go out and MAKE my fate!"

This book will show you how to make MONEY. That's the only reason it was written. I assume you would like to get rich. If you roll up your sleeves and genuinely follow its clear directions, you will become a rich, semi-retired man or woman in 10 to 12 years.

PREFACE

Sometimes the hardest thing to convince people of is the truth.

In writing this book I have been acutely conscious, in advance, of the fellow who will inevitably pick up the book, glance at it, and sagely remark, "If he knows how to make a million, why doesn't he do it? Why does he need to write a book?" Then he will smile as if he was just too smart to be fooled, and had punctured the balloon with one thrust of his incisive perception.

The answer to his natural question is in the book. You will read it and, believe me, you will know it is the truth. I hope you will follow its simple directions and make your million, too. It was written to show people like you just how to do it.

Curiously enough, there ARE people who subconsciously *do not want to get rich,* even though they declare repeatedly that that is their one ambition. When you run across the fellow who will not even bother to read what this book has to offer, you will probably find that he is one of them.

On the other hand, you are welcome to be skeptical, even doubtful, as long as you keep an open mind. That is a healthy attitude. All I ask is that you read, weigh what you read, and decide for yourself.

You picked up this book for one reason. You hoped it would show how you could become wealthy. It was precisely because of this that I chose as my publisher the one which I feel is THE most respected the world over as a dispenser of authenticated facts.

If you genuinely want to make your fortune, and are willing to read and absorb the contents of this book, putting its knowledge to work, you will one day count this moment, as you read this preface, the most momentous of your life.

TABLE OF CONTENTS

HOW TO GET RICH
IN REAL ESTATE

1

HOW IT STARTED

Let's get one thing straight. This book is 100% *fact*. There are no suppositions or "possibles" in it. It was written for a single purpose, and addressed to a certain individual. The fact that you bought the book makes you that individual. However, if you are timid, or negative, this book will not help you in the least. It's all right for you to be lazy—my kind of lazy—which was the laziness of a man who was willing to *work* at a thing dedicatedly so that he *could* enjoy laziness later and longer and in delicious, sweet idleness. But if you are too lazy to *work* at making your million, read no further. Go back and enjoy your laziness. I have no quarrel with it. This just isn't your cup of tea.

Necessarily this book will seem autobiographical. In a sense it is. That means it has got to be about me, and I hope you'll bear with that. I won't inflict any more of my personal history upon you than is necessary to give you a full background for the better understanding of my successes and failures—so that you will be able to spot the temptations that led me to some whopping mistakes—and so that you will learn the signals that say "This Way Up" to guide you to your million.

Perhaps the personal history will help you in another important phase of our undertaking—showing you how to make your million. If you see how poor I was, how little I had by special training, education, experience, or even advice, and

1

above all, how little money I had to start with, you will be more
likely to feel, "Heck! if Bob could do it with what he had, so
can I!" If we accomplish that, we've come a long way toward
success. When you believe you can do it, you have a big advantage. If you don't quite believe it, you must at least keep
an open mind, and be willing to be convinced by your own
experience. I'll do the rest, using your hands, mind and heart.

How do I know I can show you how to make your million?
Simple. I've *done* it in many cases. Some years ago Arthur C.
came in to talk to me. He had come over from the old country
and worked in a chain store as a fruit and vegetable man. He
made $17 per week. His lunch usually consisted of a discarded
tomato that had the rotten side sliced off and a roll. Total cost,
2¢. Arthur said to me, "Bob, I want to do what you are doing.
Will you help me?" Until then it had never occurred to me
that the things I had learned could be taught to another and
that he could do the same thing. I wondered if this was possible
as I replied, "OK, Arthur, here's how you begin." Ten years
later, Arthur was close to his first million and today has far sur-
passed it. And Arthur is only one of the many! By the way, don't
worry about living as frugally as Arthur did. He didn't have to
for long, after making his start under my guidance. After Arthur
there were many others.

It IS feasible for any sincere man or woman who is steadfast
in purpose, and is free of the 3 cardinal faults, Timidity, Negativeness and (immediate) Laziness to learn how and DO IT!
Here's the suggestion that I urge upon you. Let's make the
right start now. It is, in simple words: *Determine to Believe.*
Make up your mind now to push doubt aside every time it rears
its head! Doubt is the one thing that will certainly cloud your
viewpoint in all that is written here. Your absorption of the contents of this book will be impaired and the physical results seriously slashed. You virtually bar success forever.

Let's tackle our task.

Sunday was a day of rest in our house. We took to our bikes,
although where I got the energy for 80 mile bike rides I still
can't understand when I see my 6-foot sons take the car to go

two blocks. When I went to bed, I would dream before dropping off to sleep. Since my working day was devoted to the pursuit of money, my natural dreams of castles-in-air concerned acquiring a great deal of it in a less painfully laborious way. I would envision the beautiful homes we passed along Commonwealth Avenue as we roared through the trees in the open streetcars to Norumbega Park. *Somebody* had the money to live in them, I reasoned, and they'd acquired that money some way. I was going to find that way and use it. I had a goal. I wanted to have an income of $200 a week. That seemed a princely income. There were hundreds of plans evolved in those half-sleeping hours whereby that $200 would be spent. The imagined fun was ten times greater than the reality.

There was a seemingly unimportant thing in my childhood that had a powerful influence on my later life in the making of my million. On occasional Sundays, my father would take me to visit Aunt Toby in Brighton. Aunt Toby would often remark, "We've been living here 38 years and we pay $30 a month and that landlord hasn't spent one cent on this place!"

Address yourself to that remark with your most attentive eye and mind!

Mark it well, for here lies the basis of all that you are to learn in this book. The figures that Aunt Toby had named interested me but mildly at first. It only took a few minutes to multiply $30 a month by 12 months. Then $360 by 38 years. Could that be right? *Thirteen thousand six hundred eighty dollars?* Aunt Toby had paid $13,680 just to *occupy* that flat? And she had nothing material to show for it but a sizeable collection of rent receipts. Father confirmed the facts and figures. Then I asked him what the whole 6-family building was worth. "Oh, about $8,000." What expenses had the landlord had? "Well, the taxes are about $100 a year." The thirteen thousand promptly dropped to $10,680. What else? "Water, insurance, repairs, mortgage." But figure it as you may, one glaring fact stood out. Aunt Toby had paid for the building during her stay there, *and she was only one of six tenants!!*

These figures and facts whirled in my mind for months. I was never to forget them. I felt certain that this was the way to my million.

Nothing has happened since then to change that conviction.

Before we leave Aunt Toby, it is highly significant that we examine minutely the implications of another question that I'd ask my father. "If Aunt Toby isn't satisfied with the flat, why has she lived there all these years?"

He replied with a shrug, "Oh, they all gripe, but they all stay. It costs money to move, and she wouldn't do any better anyway."

I never forgot that.

Thirty years later I was checking the title of another building, just like the one Aunt Toby lived in, but much older and shabbier. I ran across the name of a former owner, one Mrs. McGee, for the tenth time in checking titles of these properties. Someone had told me that Joe M. was a descendant of the McGees, and I asked him about them. He told me of these McGees. They'd come over from Ireland, poor and illiterate. Mrs. McGee had set about to acquire property while McGee worked at a menial job. They saved as much of the poor pay as they could to invest in still another "Aunt Toby" building. Joe quoted one of Mrs. McGee's favorite remarks. We shall see later that she was very wise, and we shall see why they became very wealthy. This remark will be an important guide of policy for you as it has been for me. There was profound wisdom in it. When word reached her that a tenant was dissatisfied or had asked for an improvement, with or without the threat of moving if refused, she would reply, "They stays to suit themselves, and if they don't be suited they goes."

2

FIRST BUYS

My first job was in a grocery store. My boss put me to work filling little cartons, each with a dozen of eggs from a crate. There were red cartons and blue ones. Both were packed from the same crate. The red were then marked 39¢ and the blue ones 59¢. That was enough for me. I left the grocery business forever.

In the next eight years I did everything from shovel snow to selling cars. September 1929 found me owning a little lock and bike shop in Brookline, Massachusetts and commuting from my home some 20 miles away. A month later the depression struck and it was a struggle to keep head above water. Casting about for ways to keep the business going I started a 24-hour service in keys and locks, and advertised it extensively. This necessitated living nearer the shop and I bought my first piece of real estate—with $200 down, a first mortgage to the Brookline Cooperative bank for $2,000, and a second mortgage for $400 to the seller.

Of course, it was mostly on freezing, sleety nights that people lost their car keys in the snow or broke them off in a frozen lock. They would phone me at 3 A.M. and I would stumble out of bed, gather my tools and go out and earn the precious $3. Nevertheless I persisted in my determination to develop the business and opened several branches in supermarkets, in Boston's North Station Terminal, and even had one "branch" man-

ager operate on the fender of his car. We rigged a key machine
to his fan belt and he hawked the keys quite successfully.

Meanwhile I kept an eye open for more real estate. The
house at 171 High Street, next door to my home, became available and I bought that one. Then I heard that the 3-family
Aunt Toby around the corner at 7 High Street Place was abandoned, and I sought out its owner, Mr. W. We settled on $3,000
as a price, with $250 down and Mr. W. held the mortgage.

In a few months I had put the building into liveable condition, and rented the flats at $22 per month. That was money in
those days. The building next door, at 9 High Street Place, was
owned by a Mr. F. He approached me about it and I bought
that one for $3,400. The down payment was $300, the first
mortgage $2,500, and Mr. F. took the second mortgage for the
remaining $600.

Of course I was extremely busy between the properties, the
shop, and the branches. Yet I found time to start a small factory
where we manufactured 3-wheel bikes for peddling and delivery. Then the roof fell in. Three significant things happened
within a short space of time.

At one of my branches, in a supermarket, the owner had a
long talk with my employee. I do not know whose original idea
it was, the employee's or the owner's, but they threw out my
concession and put in their own. Soon after, the owner in-
structed the employee to teach another employee how to make
keys so that the stand could be covered at lunch hour. Of
course, the employee soon found himself out on the street. And
I did some deep thinking.

The second incident occurred when I got a call from a man
who had a brown Pontiac on Route 3. He had locked his keys in
his car. Yes, he would pay the $5. I sent out my locksmith to
do the job. He returned some 45 minutes later with the report
that the man had apparently found his keys and had left before
the locksmith got there. This was an occupational risk, and I
shrugged and sent the man out on another call. A few minutes
later a brown Pontiac pulled up at the door and the owner came
in to the shop. "Your man just charged me $5 for opening my

car, and I don't want it to happen again. Please make me three extra keys."

The third incident involved the delivery bike that my little factory was producing. I had a patent, of course. However, a welder came to the plant, bought a bike, and then told me he was going to manufacture them in his shop. I hurried to my patent lawyer, fire in my eye. Shock number three came when the lawyer told me that the patent was little protection. Yes, I could sue, but it would be years before we got a decision, and it was dangerous to restrain the welder because we might lose the suit and then be liable for heavy damages. I closed the bike factory.

In recent years when business men have come to me to learn a *better* way to make their fortunes, they have put my experience into words. Some have said they are fed up with the two big L's, Larceny and Labor. Others say, "When another must handle your money, it's no good." And, "When I am forced to sit down with a representative who will dictate how I am to run my company—or else—it makes the whole business revolting to me." That is why they swing over to real estate, where labor and leakage headaches are at an inconsequential minimum.

In the light of the incidents above, I did some sober thinking and evaluating. The amount of attention that the Aunt Tobys required was so small that I would often have forgotten they existed except that the rents coming in on the first of the month were sorely needed. Again and again these rents saved the day for me. Many a payroll that I had to pay could not have been met but for the rents. The pressing bills that the shop just didn't seem to produce enough for, were often paid by the rents.

Even more startling was the realization of where the down payments for most of the properties had come from. It was obvious that the monthly mortgage payments on the buildings came from the buildings themselves. But the pyramiding had been financed by the same source! When I had evaluated these facts, I made up my mind. I closed all the remaining branch shops.

My course was now clear.

3

FIRST BONERS

From that day, I had one main purpose in my business life. I wanted to acquire enough property to give me the income and lazy life. That was my goal. There were a few more digressions into other fields of endeavor but these were tried mainly because I could at the moment find no available means to further my main purpose—the completion of my real estate portfolio.

The very nature of real estate owned for income and pyramiding is that:

AS EACH DAY PASSES, YOU MAKE MONEY

You do not have to DO anything to create the income. It just happens by itself. Not that I am implying for a moment that it is entirely work-free. It isn't, of course. But it *goes on* making money for you, day in, day out, month by month, year by year, *by itself*. In that respect it's just like having blue-chip stocks. Of course, in stock investments, the income is being earned daily without your slightest attention. But it's rarely over five or six per cent. That means you've got to have some $200,000 to make $200 a week at five per cent. Stocks involve another factor. *All* of your dividends are fully taxable. That makes your chances of *multiplying* and pyramiding practically impossible. Not so in real estate investments. We shall learn in a later

8

chapter the amazing and *unique* tax advantages that real estate owners and operators enjoy. These special tax exemptions and benefits, combined with the other advantages, are what make it possible to make your million here as in no other field.

I resolved that I would keep an eagle-eye open for more investments and try to build up a down-payment from the income of the buildings I had.

One day I phoned Mr. W. and asked him what else he had for property in Brookline. Well, there was the 18-apartment building on Pond Avenue. How much? Oh, about $9,000. I hurried over to look at the building. In retrospect, I fear that I had sold myself even before I saw it. You see, I was looking at the building through the eyes of a man who wanted very badly to own a lot of real estate. It was that anxiety that beclouded my judgment. What's more, I had never been burnt. Everything I'd bought was making money, some more and others less. But all were doing well. After a cursory examination of the building, and a hasty reckoning of the potential income with the projected rent raises that I would make, the investment looked like a gold mine. In a matter of hours I had made an appointment with Mr. W. and had settled on a price of $8,500 with 10 per cent down. The balance was a very easy mortgage plan and I was aglow. Now I was really on my way. But just what I was on my way *to*, I did not yet know. I had a delightful orgy of figuring. Life looked good. My heart sang, "Dear old million of mine, here I come."

No sooner had I gobbled up Pond Avenue than I ran into a woman who was treasurer of the local Cooperative bank. Did they have any reasonable property of this kind? Yes, the one on Brook Street. I hurried to Brook Street and saw a brick 3-decker that seemed a steal at $4,250, and the terms were terrific. Just $250 down and the rest on mortgage. A few minutes with the pencil and I could hardly wait to close the deal. Now came my first and biggest spanking. I hope that here you will take my bitter lesson to heart and avoid this mistake as you would the plague. It is my biggest single "don't." If you will only learn the lesson here, rather than by making the mistake I did, you will have absorbed the most basic and inviolable truth in Real Estate.

Let me say it in still another way for emphasis. The factor that I overlooked in my enthusiasm is easily far and away the most important single factor determining the price, value, desirability, profit, headache—and just about every other thing that counts in the choosing and holding of a piece of real estate. This applies to *every* piece of real estate. It includes *everything* from a little 3-room hut to the biggest development tract in the country. It is impossible to over-emphasize the importance of this most vital factor.

It is LOCATION.

4

LEARNING THE FACTS OF LIFE

In the past ten years I have been called upon, perhaps 1000 times professionally and as a "friendly courtesy," to advise others on the purchase of real estate. If there has been one outstanding and common error, and there most certainly has, it has been that the prospective buyers either played down or, in some cases, entirely overlooked the most important requirement and element of all good real estate evaluation. It has happened countless times. The client or friend comes to me with a slip of paper bearing figures on a property. He wants me to say it's a marvelous buy.

He starts to espouse the fine features, the "clear profit" that his figures show. I am unimpressed. As soon as he sums up with "what do you think?" I am ready with my standard opener. "Be honest now, precisely how good is the location?" In the next ten seconds I have my answer to how I am going to advise on this one. If he begins with pursed lips, or a faraway look as he gropes for words that will not be too prejudiced, and will still be not too far from the truth, "depending on your viewpoint," I know he is covering up for a poor location. It figures. After all, he has been offered a "bargain." The figures "prove it." That's what he thinks. But unfortunately the figures *never* prove it. Not in this vital regard.

The reason he has been offered a bargain MUST be suspect. Nobody gives anything away, least of all an owner of a piece of real estate that is making good money. Therefore, we must examine it minutely to see WHY he is offering so much for so little. Please do not take the above to mean that there are never good buys. And do not conclude that there are not good bargains occasionally. In fact there are. There are even occasional fantastic buys. We will treat of them here in due time. But generally when anything is being sold for *far* less than its seeming worth, you must examine it carefully. That is simple common sense.

Thus when the friend says, "We-e-ell—I wouldn't say it's really *bad,*" I know the answer. It shortens things. I throw the burden right back at him. "My advice is that if you are sure the location is good, buy it." Of course this leaves the fellow with no more help than when he came in. But it's his own doing. He knows what's right. He simply is trying to convince himself he's found a bargain when he hasn't. You must resolve here and now, unshakably, that you will never let yourself be blinded to truth about location by the aura of the lure of the bargain or big profit it is made to look. You must never relax this vigilance. It will make or break you.

In the course of the next two years I went through hell. As the punishments of buying poor location gradually increased their pressure on me, I fought back. I had invested my bitterly accumulated mite. I dreaded accepting the conviction that I had erred. The finger pointed and said, "You goofed! This is *not* the way." I *desperately* slapped that finger aside and shouted angrily, "I will *make* it good. I will *make* it be the way!"

In many ways this may be compared to the basic training **a** soldier goes through. It is the training designed to change the individual's thinking and actions to a new and different concept and path. And it's a punishing thing. There is much resentment and rebellion against the truths of this new way of life that are being thrust upon you. Many a new draftee or enlisted man has written his friend from basic training camp, "This is HELL!" It is. And it needn't be for you. You see, I came out of training having learned only one thing. All that flailing away at the stone wall, all that spanking and disciplining I took, only left me with one piece of information. That was the sum total of the entire experience. You shall have that piece of information *without* the pain. Try your best *not* to learn it the hard way as I did. It will at least delay your rise to your million. It may completely bar you from it. It is this: *Never* compromise on location. It must be Good-location-or-I'm-not-interested— period.

In time I was forced to admit the truth. Sure, I was a fighter. I didn't give up on anything if I still could stand up. But this I couldn't lick. As I tried to inventory and evaluate, certain remarkable things thrust themselves into view for my amazed consideration. You too, should examine these as I did, for your elementary basic education.

I had three good properties and three bad ones. The three on High Street and High Street Place were good. The stuff on Pond Avenue, Villa Lane, and Brook Street were losing propositions—not to mention the ulcers they gave me. And this in spite of seeming contradictions. The good properties were shabbier! More, they were *obviously* shabbier. And in equipment, layout and decor, less desirable. Any housewife or even husband could see that. But, darn it, they rented quickly and *stayed* rented! Whereas you had to scratch and scrounge to find tenants for the bad properties, and when you did, they soon moved and you were hunting again. So what was the answer?

In contrast to the experience on Brook Street and the other bad ones, let us examine what happened in the same regard in the good ones.

Typically, High Street Place was in a desirable location. In 1933 Mr. R. moved in to the top floor at No. 7. He was still there with his family in 1955 when I sold the property (under very special methods that leave a long-range income-without-bother picture that will make you drool when we come to it).

Mr. B. moved into the first floor in the same house in 1933. He was a carpenter and in those lean years sought work from me at 75¢ an hour. He paid $22 per month. In 1955 when I sold the property to Mr. G., Mr. B. was still occupying the same apartment but his income had gone from some $30 per week to about $200 per week. His rent had increased with the times, too. He pays some $50 per month for the same flat. But he still lives there as I write this.

Do you see shades of the Aunt Toby experience in this? In the ensuing years, there were many many more properties that fell into the Aunt Toby class. Good location meant good income —and *steady*, unbroken income. And that's what we buy them for. When I bought No. 16, I got a list of the tenants from the seller, Mr. L. In this building the general rule as to all tenants that were considered "regulars" was 30 to 35 years occupancy. The ones who were considered recent occupants had lived there only 15 to 18 years!

In the Freeman property that was slummy and rundown when I bought it, Mrs. R. had been a tenant for 29 years and Mrs. F. still lives there, too, after 37 years. Most of the other 12 tenants have long tenancy records, too. And the buildings are shabby and have few conveniences.

Let us ask the big—and I do mean BIG—question—WHY? The answer is embodied in one single word—LOCATION.

To analyze this simply we must begin by realizing that in the ownership of real estate we are selling one of the three essential needs of life: Food, Clothing and Shelter. Let us examine how the great merchandisers of one elementary need—food— operate. When your local food supermarket puts a product on the display shelf it does so with the belief that the woman wants it and will buy it. If the store buyer does not believe that it is what the public wants, he will not stock the item. In simple terms the store is giving the consumer what the consumer wants. This principle carries through to many other parts of the chain's operation. Giving the customer what she wants is the guiding factor in deciding on many things: The style of shopping, lighting of the store, arrangement of the racks, parking facilities, choice of products offered, such as stockings, magazines and utensils. They all do the same thing—give the public what it wants. *And the food chains know the score!* I am content to learn from their methods and wisdom, for I, too, am selling an essential of life to the same consumer—shelter. The same good principles necessary to success in supplying a consumer-need apply here as well as to food.

Reduced to terms of application to my problem of inability to sell the shelter of the bad properties, I was trying to sell the consumer something it didn't want, poor location. Sometimes the supermarket might put a product on the shelves experimentally to test public reaction. Some people would "try" it, then never buy it again, or return it for refund. That product would come off the shelves quickly. The chain isn't fool enough to try to sell it *simply because it can buy it at a bargain*. We in real estate shouldn't be that stupid either.

When we are offered a bargain in real estate we must never forget that we are not buying something *we* are going to consume, we are buying WHAT we are going to be *offering* to the *public*.

If we are to avoid the unenviable position of owning a thing for sale and being unable to find a customer for it, we must devote our best judgment to the points about the property that will most influence the acceptability of our product (shelter) when we offer it for sale. And the most important single feature of ALL property is location! Hence when you start looking over a proposition, examine the most important thing first. Put yourself in the place of a supermarket buyer who is considering buying a warehouse-full of a certain style of canned beans. Let us say these beans are ill-smelling but usable. Would the fact that the price is very low overcome the fact that you know something about these beans that makes it reasonably certain that you will not be able to sell them? Are you planning to eat a million cans of beans yourself? No! You are buying something for the single purpose of selling it!

The difficulty of selling the shelter in bad locations is comparable to the difficulty in selling beans that smell, or taste horrible. If you see the thing in that light, you need never err in this regard. Irrespective of HOW the figures seem to prove it is a good proposition, you do not want it. The figures may be compared to those that are presented to the market buyer. The owner of the beans shows him that the beans may be sold at price lower than current market, and still leave a fat profit to the store. The buyer simply will not buy it. Neither should you be tempted by the figures.

So much for the factor of location. Since it pervades our thinking and is an absolute governor of results, we have emphasized it by good and by horrible example. It would be pointless to waste more time and space belaboring the point. Let us examine further steps in our journey.

5

DUMPING THE DEADWOOD

It was time to stand back, appraise and admit the folly of the three bad choices. No sooner did a tenant move in than he was looking for another place. Only a fool would persist and beat his brains against a stone wall by trying to make the public accept what it didn't want. So I set about unloading the bad ones. I advertised. I talked them up. I passed the word around. Soon this produced results. Others wanted to own income-producing real estate, and had not learned the lesson that still had my head spinning. Mind you, these were depression times. The amount of ready cash was the all-important point in *all* business. So I tried to make the things attractive by small down payments. This worked fine. By the way, in the intervening years nothing has happened to change my mind about this as a wonderful method in selling real estate— particularly real estate that is otherwise hard to sell.

In talking to one (we'll call him) Farrow, I said, "I've got one piece of real estate that I'll sell for a ten-cent cigar!" Mr. Farrow was a bit of a wise guy. He thought he had me caught in a legally binding offer. He pressed his point. "Where?" I answered, "The brick house at 114 Brook Street." Quickly he took me up on it. "OK. It's a deal. I'll take it," and he smirked in his triumph.

So we sat ourselves down and made a contract! Right then and there. For and in consideration of one ten-cent cigar. I actually sold all my right, title and interest in and to the real estate situated at 114 Brook Street, Brookline, Mass.—a brick 3-family house, occupied by 3 tenants, for one ten-cent cigar. Believe it or not, to this day I firmly believe I stuck him. He took over the mortgage, signed up on a new note, handed me the cigar (which I still have framed, as a reminder of what NOT to do in Real Estate) and he marched down to the building and informed the tenants that he was the new owner and would be around the first of the month for the rent. He got a bit of a surprise.

The tenants had news for him. They gave *him* notice that by the first of the next month they would move out! This fazed him only a little. He had so little invested that it still didn't seem possible that he had taken on a loser. But he learned. In the ensuing years, while he hung on trying to make the public accept something it didn't want, he learned something that I had paid heavily to learn. I heard he was trying to sell it from time to time, and then lost track of the whole painful affair. By the way, I don't smoke.

It was time to push the unloading of the other boner—The Pond Avenue-Villa Lane Group. To anyone who had not learned his elementary lesson, the figures were mighty attractive. They were so attractive that you could easily overlook the slummy location. And I finally found a customer who did. Here again the allure of a low down payment—really a token amount —sold the property. The idea of owning an 18-apartment unit in Brookline, Mass. (a highly desirable residential town) with only $1000 down was too much for Mr. J. He beat the down payment figure from $1000 to $500, and I let him win. He assumed the old mortgage of some $7,700 and signed a second mortgage to me of $500, which he eked out in time and paid off.

When I had finally gotten rid of these properties, I licked my wounds and contemplated the future. The depression had brought business to new lows, and then established even lower lows. Still, people had to have shelter. Many who owned properties in the deluxe class (for those times) were suffering.

Their $75 and $100-a-month tenants had moved into my $30 and $40 flats. The deluxe apartments stood vacant, and these vacancies brought attendant worries. In order to keep from losing the building to the mortgagee, they HAD to have rental income to keep up the payments, or at least pay enough to forestall foreclosure. So the owners started to improvise inducements to get tenants to move into their buildings. You would see ads offering "free rent for 6 months" or "will pay your moving costs" and the like. Even without saying so, it was assumed the owner would completely redecorate. That was standard in the demands of new tenants. Of course these measures imposed new burdens of themselves. It cost a substantial amount of money to redecorate an apartment throughout. Things got so bad among the big owners that they were driven, in this and many other localities, to form associations. The prime purpose of these was to agree among themselves to abandon the practices that were pyramiding with each owner trying to outbid the other until it became absurd. To some extent these measures worked, but it fell far short of solving the problem for many.

However, these troubles never brushed me. I owned what the public wanted. I offered the public the shelter at a price it could afford to pay and a location it wanted to live in. As soon as I learned a few more lessons in management (which we will discuss later), I reduced vacancies *and* bad debts to less than 3 per cent of the gross! This was not only unheard of, but unthinkable in those days, and still is, in the trade generally. But it is perfectly possible for any other to achieve this fine record if he knows:

> What to buy (and what to stay away from),
> Where to buy,
> How to finance,
> How to manage.

You will learn these things well in this book.

6

WHAT IS THE BEST BUY
IN REAL ESTATE AND WHY

Let us draw a sad, slow curtain over the bad choices I made in those days and begin to specify the *right* beginning for your guidance.

I will assume you are a small investor, and that you have only $2,500 to $3,000 to invest. If you have more you can speed the process and get started quicker, pyramid more quickly, and reach your goal sooner. But you cannot improve on the method unless you have phenomenal luck—and we're not planning on that. Our method is based on a universal public need for one of the essentials of life and our ability to supply it at a good profit. Luck has little to do with it.

Wherever you live in the United States, you are likely to have near you some rental units of the style of Aunt Toby or their equivalent in housing. This may take the form of duplexes, row houses a la Philadelphia, or apartment buildings. Everything we say here about Aunt Tobys applies to *class of rental* and *not a type of building*.

Wherever you are, there are rental units for the average working-man. It is entirely unimportant that the FORM of the rental unit may be drastically different from the style of Aunt Toby that is commonly called a three-decker. In every part of the world I have seen that there are one or more forms of lower middle class or workingman's housing. They are Aunt Tobys. These buildings were built 30, 60 and even 90 years ago. Often the 90-year-olds are more profitable than the sparkling new apartment houses!

You may find workingmen's housing in your area in any one of the dozen forms. But you can be sure it is there, and you will find that the directions here will guide you in appraising it and buying it.

In the Southwest Coastal cities, particularly Los Angeles, I have seen Aunt Tobys take several forms. Sometimes there is a four-family duplex. There are single lots on which four separated single houses have been built, each "free-standing."

In San Francisco there are many row houses, with one or two units to each house.

All of New England generally has the type of Aunt Toby from which I drew its name, three-deckers and some joined to form six-family blocks, all on one lot.

In Montreal and Quebec, the frugal French have divided their own houses that front on the street, many even putting the staircases outdoors to utilize inside space more efficiently, and then they have built an additional house, and sometimes two, on the land in back of the house—for income.

In New Orleans there are other versions. A lot is split down the center with an alley, on which several units front. Thus four, eight and often 12 or more units may be rented out on the one lot.

New Mexico has the one-story Spanish-style three-to-six apartment rows, and some have added a second story for additional units.

Baltimore and Philadelphia have the small single units, wall-to-wall, in rows, often divided into two units to a house. North Carolina has these too, and several other versions of workingmen's housing. There are some row houses in New Jersey too, but many others take the form of free-standing three-family blocks.

In Oklahoma the owner often lives in the front house, and

has divided his garage into two units. Some even add a second story to the garage for additional income.

Arizona has the adobe-type four-family arrangement, sometimes remodelled from a large garage.

Detroit has the large multiple-unit apartment house in many sizes and varieties. In St. Louis two two-family units are paired. We are concerned with *figures—income*, not the form of the building. Whatever shape or form the Aunt Tobys in your area take, the principle is the same and we need only treat here of the one type that is reasonably typical all over the country, in Canada and many foreign countries. Let us examine this unique piece of architecture. The ordinary three-family house has, let us say, 17 rooms. Five on the first floor and six each on the second and third floors. When it was built, probably in the 20's or before, it cost perhaps $12,000 or, as a general rule-of-thumb, $600 per room. Those were the days when carpenters got 75¢ per hour or less, and the bricklayers approximately the same. Laborers who dig, tote, carry and clean, rated some 50¢ per hour.

Today that same house would cost, as a general average, throughout the country, about $5,000 to $6,000 per room. That makes a total cost of $85,000 to $102,000 for the house. Today that same bricklayer or carpenter gets $80 per day and there are very heavy "pluses" above that. For example there is the item of insurance. The builder who employs roofers must sustain an insurance cost on each roofer of a very high percentage of the roofer's salary, which must be paid to the insurance company for workmen's compensation insurance, over and above the salary to the roofer himself. What's more, the builder MUST carry this insurance in almost all states. And just as an added headache—it is very difficult for the builder to GET the insurance even though he wants to pay for it. The insurance companies simply do not want the business.

In addition, there are the modern building codes. These require many expensive fire and other protections which old laws did not require Hence it is easy to see why the building that cost $12,000 in 1922 would now cost eight to twelve times as much, with little change as far as the rentable quality is affected.

Now when a piece of real estate (inclusive of land and buildings) costs $85,000 as the keys are handed over, ready for occupancy, there is a general rule of thumb as to what that building should produce as an income. This has long been established and is pretty broadly accepted. The accepted custom is 15 per cent of the total cost, as rent, per year. That is another way of saying that when a builder invests in a piece of land and puts a building on it, he is generally entitled to get all his investment back in about six to seven years. That is gross income, of course, and does not take into account his necessary expenditures.

Following that rule of thumb, the three-decker of today would have to fetch some $12,700 per year as total income before expenses to justify its cost of erection. That figures out to $4,000 per apartment or some $330 per month rent for each. Obviously, there would be little, if any, market for such flats as this at such a rental. That leads us to a conclusion. It is this: present replacement cost of a standard three-family house is so high that we can rely on this truism: *no more will be built.* This for the simple reason that it would be economically preposterous as an investment.

Having established this conclusion, let us examine the investment of a three-family with an eye on the fact that those that now exist will be the last of their kind. That is very important. It means that we will never have competition from any new units of the type we have. Such competition for the consumer's shelter dollar as we will have will be limited to other fields, such as the desire to own a single house, the desire of the tenant to own his own three-decker and *collect rent* instead of paying it out, and such improvement in the tenant's circumstances as move him to raise his living quarters' standards as his economic status improves. We will see that all three are negligible.

For one thing, a half-century of broad experience shows clearly that as a class, the three-family tenant *remains* one for decades, until death or some other drastic family upheaval dis lodges him. Even then, in most cases, the married son or daughter, and in many cases the widow herself, continues on as a tenant indefinitely and the flow of income to the owner remains uninterrupted. If we were to attempt to analyze why this particular genus of tenant, above all other types, seems to stay "forever" in one flat, we will find many reasons.

To begin with, let us not forget the automobile. To most people the car (as a status symbol, or for many other reasons) seems to require a larger and larger part of his paycheck. And he often becomes a two-car supporter, also. To these people, there is a secure feeling of snugness about living in the same old place for decades. It would take much to replace that. There are not the constant needlings of the competition in housing as there are in autos to buy the more expensive product, with the possible exception of the developer of the single-house community. To him we lose a few occasionally, but it is a negligible percentage. The tenant, if he does consider buying a single, soon starts to figure how demanding a monkey he would be putting on his back in undertaking the overhead of a single and usually drops the idea.

Then there are the ever-increasing costs of the schooling of the children. Colleges are expensive, today, and almost may be said to be a luxury only the rich can afford. Where we once considered the boy who was going to college the exception, he is now the rule. And his sister usually expects a college education too. All on papa's pocketbook. This scotches any ideas about buying a house of their own.

Perhaps as powerful a "stay-put" factor is the item of the neighbors and friends he has come to enjoy around him in the same old place. The three-decker tenant is as comfortable with these as with an old shoe. He hates to change, perhaps secretly fearing the awkwardness of making new friends among other home-buyers in the development who "are maybe classier."

Add to the above the general inertia that pervades all human action, the tendency to procrastinate, and the fact that we are all perpetually a little behind the installment collector what with all the washers, freezers, and gadgets the average man is signed up for. You can readily see why he stays put. Even moving, itself, costs money. Not to mention new rugs, drapes, furniture, more expensive shopping, living up to a new house, and perhaps a second car. The idea is tossed aside. "No new house for us right now, I guess." And so it goes. And the years pass and lo! they have "lived here for 37 years and—" Aunt Toby again.

Thus when we own the three decker—we have the thing that, once wisely rented (and note carefully I said *wisely*) *usually* establishes an *unceasing income* from the tenants and this income continues beyond the belief of those who have not experienced it.

This does not obtain with any other type of rental, generally, with the possible exception of one other field, and that field is rapidly vanishing. That is the little neighborhood store. Twenty-five years ago we could say of the small store that was rented to a grocer or to a chain, this is permanent. The drug store and the tailor and shoemaker who occupied the other stores in the little local shoping center were steady tenants too. They were firmly fixed and they made a living. Thus they stayed on—for decades. But this was so only until the supermarket came into the picture. Now all that has changed.

In the past quarter century, as each big chain opened its supermarkets in "decentralized shopping areas," that is, out of the congested districts, with the generous parking and the neon-lit bright shopping in a carnival atmosphere, the same chain gradually closed its local small stores. This spelled the doom of the whole little local neighborhood store block. The chain store had been the heart of the little block. Without the traffic that the chain store pulled, the shoemaker next door soon folded, and, in time, the other little stores that depended on the same traffic followed. This was hastened by two intervening causes. First, the parking curse that these small store blocks were never designed to care for. Perhaps the tailor or the druggist parked his *own* car (as did some of the other shopkeepers) right in front of his store all day, "to have it handy for deliveries" and soon no customer could park in that area even if he wanted to. Second, the general rise that has occurred in salary levels and the drop in the storekeeper's income made him consider giving up the long hours of store-keeping in favor of the steady income and short hours of the job, working for another. And the salary was sure and dependable. So he closed up and took the job. That left another vacant store. The result was that soon the store blocks in local neighborhood areas stood empty. Investment-wise, its back was broken. Today this type of property makes a poor investment indeed.

But come decentralization or not, depression or inflation, come low priced housing developments and, in some cases, practically free housing in some governments, our business only grows better. That figures too. For we must remember that the population is constantly increasing. Thus the supply of our tenants is increasing. But the supply of our type of housing is, if anything *decreasing*.

The law of supply and demand has seen us through all these and we've made money steadily through it all. Of course it is not given to men to more than guess at the future, but based on what we see and what we have experienced it is a safe bet that the supply of *our type* of tenants will steadily increase and unless you think the bricklayers and carpenters are some day going to work for $5 per day instead of $80 it does not seem possible that the supply of housing for these tenants will ever increase in anything near the price range they want to pay.

Thus the Aunt Toby, whether in the form of a three-family or its equivalent in the various parts of the country, is unique in these regards. As such, we should set our sights to acquiring as many of them as possible, following only the strict rules that are here set out.

7

WHAT TO CHECK FIRST

There are three basic rules to follow in choosing the building you are going to invest in. The first permits of not the slightest deviation. It will be fatal to compromise on the point of location. Let us see how we test for this requirement.

Let us say you have been offered a building located on Elm Street. You go to see it. The *time of day* when you see it is even important. Don't go while children are in school. Many a street presents quite a different picture at 10 A.M. than it does at 4 P.M. Since we fear slummy locations, although we do not fear slum *buildings* since we can correct that, we see a building and its area best for our purposes when it is at its worst. Now this building is getting $100 per month as rent from each tenant. You will find it very easy to determine definitely and unmistakably whether this building passes the first test. Drive along the street, at 4 P.M. and look about as you approach the building. Remember not to decide this on the basis of whether YOU would like to live here. Just ask yourself this, "If you were going to pay $100 per month for a flat, would you consider this location satisfactory?" In the answer you will find the yes or no to location. But see to it that all the factors are considered. If there is a noisy or smelly factory nearby, or a dump or railroad, make sure you see the place, hear the place and even smell the place at its worst. Only thus can you get the full picture.

There is one more item—wet cellars. Examine the land

around the building for a few hundred yards in each direction. If any neighboring land slopes *down* to your building, be careful of the incurable curse of wet cellar and the misery that comes with it. If you are at all concerned, first examine the cellar itself, ask the lower floor tenant, and then wait for a very rainy day or spell, and go to the cellar then. If you check through in all these points, you can proceed further. Otherwise drop it. For my money there is no cure for this disease. I say this although many have stoutly maintained otherwise.

My experience is that in those cases where this handicap has been "cured" there really was never a cure, only an abatement of the misery by digging a trench just inside the leaky wall, filling it with gravel and letting the water come in and drain out again. A very doubtful cure. In the many other cases I've encountered, I've seen owners strip the soil from around the entire foundation, coat the foundation with waterproof cement and tar, and after the earth was replaced, the water seeped in as before.

Hence we peremptorily pass up the buildings that do not pass the first test, that of location. Notice that we do not ask that the location be "beautiful" or "lovely" for all buildings. Not at all. We use the yardstick that is clearly indicated by the rental rate itself. That determines the attitude and measuring eye with which we judge location.

We try to see this location through the eyes of a prospective tenant who has come to the building to see a flat. We try to see it as he will see it, and judge it as he will judge it. This is NOT difficult. We certainly can quickly dismiss the locations that are obviously so bad that even the $100 tenant will certainly not find the location to his liking. These really give us no problem nor do those that are obviously good. It is the class of location that is "borderline" that may puzzle us.

I have taught hundreds of people this principle and many have expressed doubt about their future ability to determine the fitness of those locations which were not quite bad enough to reject at a glance, and not quite good enough to approve immediately. I have learned over the years that they were worrying without cause. It just does not work out that way. We have all seen that in some principles of practice, the theory is easy to understand but the practice is difficult or even impossible. Here it is reversed. The theory may be hazy, but the practice invariably turns out comparatively simple.

There are a few simple things that will give you your answer. I speak now only of those locations that are doubtful. The first step is to ask yourself whether in your opinion, the location would be satisfactory to a prospective tenant who was considering a flat in this building at $100 (if that is the rent rate). The next step is to ask the tenants themselves, but this step must be approached with one reservation. In those cases where you are considering a building that has been "over-milked", that is, everything taken out by the landlord without putting anything back unless forced, you should approach the tenants with the mental reservation that they will probably be discontented with everything about their flats.

Thus any dissatisfaction on the part of such tenants must be weighed in the light of the general conditions which they have been forced to accept under greedy or neglectful ownership. If such a tenant were to indicate to you that he is unhappy with the LOCATION of the building, you should press him for the specific points that he finds undesirable. He may come up with some very significant answers that will bear and guide investigation before buying. But if his complaint is very general, with no specification, you may discount it, as merely a baseless item in a general group comprising unhappiness.

Here is a little point that may help you in judging this matter of location. You should give WEIGHT but not absolute control in your judgment to this point. Find out from the prospective seller, or the tenants themselves, how long they have lived there. If the general average term of occupancy for each tenant is over 5 years, you should add this to the plus side in the decision, but by itself, it should not be the determining factor. We have seen that this type of tenant will often stay put in the same apartment for decades even though discontented with the accommodations. The mere fact that a tenant recites that old refrain—"been living and paying rent here for 31 years and that landlord never spends a cent"—should not carry *any* weight with you, since it is reasonably standard and is of the same stripe as the standard griping of G.I.'s about the food. Where tenants have continued to occupy for over five years, you may assume that the accommodations are such that the location is at least adequate for that rent level. You will usually find that the tenants have, on an average, occupied much, much longer than five years, but if asked to set a minimum figure, I feel that a tenant who is *really* dissatisfied with location would not linger five years in the unhappy location.

Once Arthur C. came to my office, almost starry-eyed with a deal that he had been offered. To him, the price was the be-all and end-all of the deal. "Bob, I just saw the most astounding bargain! Nine buildings, all Aunt Tobys. Income over $17,000 and I can buy it for $65,000, with $5,000 down. What can I lose? It's a wow of a deal." Of course, you and I know WHY Arthur was offered a package which, if all were as it should be, would be worth $100,000. Something was wrong. And that something was usually location. When Arthur calmed down, I told him the experience of Mr. B. as I always do in these cases.

One day Mr. B. and I were asked to draw a set of better forms, such as tenant leases, et cetera, for the local real estate organization. We were leaving the session and he drove me to the outskirts where my car was parked. As we rode he confided that he was aglow with a buy he had just clinched.

"I had business on this certain street and I chatted with an elderly man who was working around a building. He said he owned all eight buildings. He said he was old and tired and wanted to sell out. I was really only joking when I asked, 'What will you take for the bunch?' He replied, 'Look, mister, you mean business? Listen, I'll sell you the whole group, 25 tenants, for a very low price!' "

Ben replied, "What do you call a low price?"

The elderly gentleman retorted, "What will you give me?"

Still not really serious, Ben shot back, "Give you $15,000."

"You got a deal," replied the man to a shocked Ben.

When Ben told me about it, he was elated over just one point. He, being a lawyer, knew that nothing was binding until signed up. He felt sure that when the owner told his lawyer to draw a purchase and sale agreement for such a ridiculous price, the lawyer would either (1) have the old man put away, or (2) buy it for himself.

"I never believed the deal would ever be sewed up," continued Ben, "and when we met this morning, and all went through and we signed up, I was the most surprised lawyer in Boston. Imagine, Bob, eight three-deckers, and one has a store and three flats. All tenants heat themselves, all filled up, et cetera—it's still hard for me to believe!"

I congratulated him on the "amazing bargain" but, of course, I knew who had put one over on whom in this case—and you do, too. Let us never forget *why* the old gentleman's lawyer had readily permitted him to sell at this ridiculous figure. It is by focusing our attention on the fact that the lawyer had an intimate knowledge of his client's affairs and that he consummated the deal exactly as the owner had made it orally with Ben, that we learn the lesson here.

Two months later I saw Ben in Probate Court. He looked as if he'd aged ten years. When I asked him how the new investment was going along, he peered at me.

"You knew, didn't you, Bob," he sighed, "why the thing was being sold so cheaply?"

"Well, I supposed it was the usual curse—bad location."

"It sure was," he replied, "and I'm trying to unload. I've learned a terrible lesson. There's no such thing as a price that makes up for bad location—no matter *how* low."

8

WHAT TO CHECK SECOND

The second big test for you to apply to your prospective purchase is the requirement that the rents be modest. Here again we will have no difficulty with the extremes. Let us consider first what we mean by the word modest.

Various studies over the years have established from time to time the percentage of his income that an average workman pays for shelter. In the twenties and for some time prior to that, the percentage ranged between 22 and 25 per cent. That is, you might say that when a workman earned $40 a week, he generally paid $40 per month for housing. The economists have pointed out that the three essentials of life were vital to him and that he had an outlook on spending that was far different from what it is today.

He also had different *values*. To him, it was *worth* one-fourth of his paycheck to live in that flat, although he knew he could buy less desirable shelter for his family for perhaps half that. Owning an automobile was not as important to him as living in that flat, if he had to choose between the two. Also owning the auto had not been made as easy by way of installments. His neighbor did not own a car either and there seemed to be no such compulsion to live up to the Joneses as obtains now.

There were several other things that governed his spending. For one, his attitude toward what he considered the luxuries of living. Inconceivable as that may seem today, there were actually things which he *felt he could not afford!* And he cheerfully got along without them. This attitude was partially engendered by another factor.

He had no assurance that the future would take care of itself, that he could never starve. In those years, the working man faced the grim reality that you enjoyed only that which you earned, and you had to provide for your own future and old age. Perhaps he would not have accepted an assurance of what he considered charity even if available. So he lived within what he felt were his means, and was content. Now all that has changed, and I include *all* of that.

Today's workingman sees his old age provided for, hence, the necessity to provide for it removed. He lives to the limit, and with a small percentage of exceptions, saves very little of his income. (We're getting close to the point that affects us now.) He values the essentials of life quite differently than he used to. His car is more important, and he trades it frequently for a newer model. He spends on recreation, hobbies, the children's education, and other things now that he used to feel he should do without.

As a result, with his limited paycheck, some things must be slashed. And there is just where we come in. We provide him with the class and location of shelter that he wants at the price he *wants* to pay. And today he wants to pay a far smaller portion of his income for shelter. Thus the workman of today only spends some 12 to 15 per cent of his paycheck for shelter as contrasted with 35 years ago; *and we are the only ones who can supply it.*

What's more, in the foreseeable future it is hard to see how there will be any change in our monopoly. If there is any way in which competition for that rent dollar is going to be created, it must come to pass by means we consider virtually impossible. That is, again, bricklayers and carpenters working for $6 a day instead of $80 and $90 per day. Yes, and then there's government housing, federal, state, and municipal.

Government housing has been a comparative failure. It was born and based on the premise that if you take people out of the slums and put them in nice housing, they will live up to the new environment. When many of these people lived in the slums, they used their bathtubs for coalbins, gin or what not. Now that they have been "elevated" and relocated they use the entire building for even worse purposes, and any observer can see the truth of this in thousands of places.

I have had dozens of tenants who came to live in my buildings, disgusted after a few months of sampling what the government was offering through public housing. It must be remembered that our tenants are nice people—clean people and good-living Americans. They have no wish to destroy that which the government supplies free. They use soap on their children and, when necessary, a strap. Illegitimacy is still a disgrace among them, not an envied means of getting more welfare allowance. So they come to us for the housing they want and we supply it.

If we wanted to set a norm for the amount a workman earns, we would have to leave a substantial range for the various parts of the country. But let us try to analyze a fairly standard average. Say your tenant works on the assembly line in an auto plant. He makes some $3.50 per hour for 40 hours, or grosses $140 per week. Of course, there are deductions and withholdings, but there is also overtime pay. In addition there is usually some income being brought into the family either by the wife through part-time work or by a grown son or daughter.

Thus the family can usually plan on $160 or $180 per week clear. This makes the monthly income some $680 to $750 and if he spends 15 per cent of that for his rent, he is content. And so are we.

By these calculations, it becomes apparent why in my experience in these times with present-day figures and habits (as well as those of past decades) the shelter that we had to offer had plenty of takers at the price. And it also explains why my vacancy percentage was so infinitesimal a part of the picture. It has been my experience that there are 100 prospective tenants for a $110 flat to each tenant seeking $200 quarters. It boils down to this. Our American workman wants decent quarters (not lux) at about $100 to $125 per month and is willing to foot his own heat bill besides. Therefore we call that "modest rent." You will have no difficulty determining the range covered by the words "modest rent" in your area.

9

WHY WE PREFER
UNHEATED PROPERTIES

There is just one more feature which we will seek in our investment picture. That is, the arrangement under which the tenants supply their own heat. It may be unnecessary for me to expound on this, but experience has shown that this one curse in property management and the processing of complaints, by itself, outweighs all others combined, and by some 10 or 20 times over.

Owners have estimated that of all the complaints they receive in the management of their properties, 95 per cent have to do with heat. My own experience bears this out, beyond question. I realize that there are areas, as in central New York City, where virtually all accommodations include heat supplied by the owner, but these are usually not the type we are seeking anyway, and they are not in our price range.

In choosing the properties in which we are going to invest, we seek those where a minimum of attention on our part will be required. We are directing our investor's eye toward a *different class of property*. We prefer not to own the type of property that generally includes heat or janitor service with the rent. The type (or class) of tenant who seeks the heated, janitor-serviced apartment is a *different* tenant from those we seek. He is much more transient, often moving to a new place each year. And he has an *attitude* about the owner (or the owner's representative—the janitor). This tenant expects the owner to stand by and be available 24 hours a day and 7 days a week to jump at his beck and call. If a window shade sticks, or he has dropped a washcloth into the sink, he "sends for the janitor" with the full assumption and expectation that the janitor will take care of it. He would be indignant if he were refused. The tenant we seek has no such attitude. I have spoken to some prospective tenants over the years who were considering my flats. When I sensed from their conversations that they were accustomed to this type of attention and service I politely urged them to rent a heated apartment with janitor service. I confessed that my flats were for folks who would shift for themselves. A favorite expression was "in my buildings, I give you just one thing—the key to the door, and you must do just about everything else for yourself. If there are any electric or plumbing repairs (except plugged drains), or roof leaks, I will attend to them. But beyond that you are on your own." I never had any trouble getting tenants. Conversely, I often had to reject an application because, even though the applicant was avowedly willing to assume the rules of my buildings, I felt that he would not be contented and permanent. It was the permanent tenant that I wanted, and I always had plenty to choose from.

There are, of course, various types of heating equipment, and in some areas, flats of our type have no need for heating at all. But the third desired feature remains unchanged. We prefer to own buildings where the tenants furnish their own heat. There is another factor that is in our favor when we are free of this curse. The rising costs. Every so often there is a crisis of one kind or another and fuel prices soar. It is just not practical to raise the rent each time the price of furnace oil rises one cent per gallon. When the tenant is paying for it, he alone is concerned. We can lease a flat to a tenant for many years, and fear no ingredient cost that will seriously cut our net (with the exception of taxes). As to taxes, we provide for this by a so-called escalator clause in long leases. It takes into account any increase in the tax bill of the building and adds a fair proportion of such increase to the rent automatically.

In addition to the increases in costs of fuel, let us mention the occasional strikes and other occurrences that completely shut off the supply of fuel. On these occasions the landlord is, in some states, in a very unenviable position. The law says he MUST keep the flats warm (in those buildings where he furnishes heat), ignoring the fact that he just cannot buy oil. Sometimes owners have made a hurried, if not panicky, conversion to coal and thus tried to keep from getting into trouble, but their position is far from easy.

Another factor inherent in the heated building is that of labor. Where coal is the fuel, there are myriad headaches attendant. The janitors go on strike, and the owner finds himself wielding the coal-shovel. Or there is a strike of truckdrivers, or railroad strike, maritime strike, or what have you. Any of these puts the building into an emergency.

A final misery is the matter of degree and period of heat. The norm in heating apartments is 70 to 72 degrees during the hours between 7 A.M. and 11 P.M. But there are workers who want to rise and dress before 7 and these invariably want the owner to get the apartment (which means the whole building) warm by 6 or even 5 A.M. Of course, some tenants like to stay awake and watch the late show or the late late show on TV nowadays and want the apartment warm into the wee hours too. As long as they are not paying for it, they can see no reason why they are not entitled to it.

This same headache is felt as to dates of heating. Some thin-blooded tenants want heat even in August, if there is a damp or cool day. Others protest loudly if the owner shuts the heat off on June 1.

Then there is the tenant who works in an office which is kept at 80 degrees all day. When the tenant gets home to an apartment that is 72, he or she is "freezing" and soon lets the owner know about it. It is very hard to reason with a person who is miserable with cold, even though the apartment temperature is right. Summing up on this point, you will find that the tenant who is paying for his heat is content with 70 when, if he were living in a heated apartment, he would be complaining at 75 degrees because "that living room radiator is cold." But if he were paying for it he would don a sweater on a cool September or October day rather than start up the heating system for the winter.

Thus, because of the headaches, expense, worries, night-calls, wars, strikes, labor troubles, we try to avoid property that requires us to furnish heat to the tenants. That is our third factor.

In the early years of my ownership an incident in which I almost made a fatal error may serve to exemplify an interesting point. I had just bought two three-family buildings that shared a party wall. Each tenant heated his own flat by coal furnace. So imbued with enthusiasm was I with my new purchase that I got "new owner's disease." That is, I overdid the attention to the thing. I sought out ways to "improve" or change. In this mood, I got an idea.

I called on each tenant with this proposition: I started with the statement that "you now pay $22 per month." Then I pointed out that in heating for himself the tenant shoveled coal, nursed a furnace, sifted ashes, lugged barrels out to the curbstone for the trash wagon, and in addition, the tenant heated his own needed hot water for all purposes. I asked what the tenant spent for coal each year. "Oh, about 6 tons—$72." "Okay," said I, moving in with the clincher, "suppose I were to install a central heating system and keep your apartment warm. There would be no more work on your part, no ashes, no cold spells, perfect comfort throughout the house. And I'll charge you just what you are paying—$6 a month more on the rent. What's more, I'll throw in constant supply of hot water too!" This tenant replied, "Raise my rent to $28? Oh, no, I couldn't afford that! Maybe $25, but that would be my limit."

I was a little groggy from this interview as I knocked on the door of another tenant in the same building. I went through the same explanation of the projected plan. I got substantially the same answer! I left the building in a haze. Of course I never made the installation and those tenants stayed in that flat at that rent for years, until the forties, when things began to rise generally.

One day I told the incident to a banker in that town. He and his father before him had acquired a thorough knowledge of the *thinking* of people. He grinned at me. "I hope you learned your lesson. These folks *want* a flat of the kind you have, and want to feel that they are paying $22 rent—and that's it—period. Don't monkey with it. You ought to have your head examined for even considering improving their lot." I did not soon forget his lesson. From then on I stuck to giving the people what the people want, not what *I* think they should have.

You can summarily dismiss any property that does not fulfill the two basic requirements of modest rent and decent location. As to heat, we try to buy those that are tenant-heated, if possible.

10

THE TIME IS NOW

In the next step in learning how you are going to get rich, you must be careful to avoid negativeness more than ever. I have been asked to start many men and women along my path. But I have noticed that if they were at all negative, it showed up in this phase of the endeavor. Perhaps the psychologists would analyze this as a secret but real desire on the part of the subject NOT to get rich but to continue to wallow in mediocrity. I early learned the fable of the cave and the robe. It best demonstrates my point.

You have seen it in the experience with the tenants who were offered heat in the previous chapter. The story goes: Once, way back in prehistoric times there were two men who each occupied a cave in the side of a mountain. Each summer they would hunt and fish and live quite comfortably. But each winter they would huddle in their bearskin robe and shiver and wait for spring again. To one cave-dweller, the robe and the gloomy cave spelled shelter and some measure of protection against the elements—and life. The other was a little more aggressive. He came to his neighbor and proposed, "Let us leave this misery and go down into the valley. We cannot be much worse off. Perhaps we may find a better life." But the other replied, "Oh, no, go away with your mad ideas. I *have* this cave and this robe, and I wouldn't think of leaving them. If I did, who knows, I might suffer terribly and be even colder. Then I'd

41

wish I had my cave and robe back, and I might have lost them. Oh, no, go away."

So when, after a few weeks of more or less desultory hunting, the report comes that "guess there are no more like that to be had," I know we've got another fizzle in this one. After all, *every single one* of the men and women whom I've started and who had the right attitude is doing famously. I need only glance at their records to be positively reassured that the field is still ripe and rich with opportunity for those who are *positive* and not negative. For those who really, down deep, *want* to venture forth from the security of the little they have— their cave and robe. It soon shows.

So I ask you to approach this whole venture with certain attitudes. They are absolutely essential if you are to succeed. Let us begin with the first plaintive excuse for a withdrawing cave-dweller.

"You bought at the right time. It's too late now."

I have found that it does no good to prove to this fellow how wrong he is. He wants out, without losing face. In his view, 1946 was too late, and *every* year is either too late or "not the right time." So I wave him on. Let us look at the record.

True, I started to build my portfolio of holdings just when the depression started. But when the forties began and things started to get better, all things rose at once! The prices of the buildings went up—so did the rents, so the net is bigger than ever. It cost more to fix a roof and the tax bill was up. But so was the income, and each principle remained the same as in 1930, 1935 and 1939. The proportions were much the same. Only the figures were changed. The same formula was sound in 1946, as it was in 1936 and 1956. If there was a variation in this area it lay in our favor. One big item did *not* rise in proportion to other things. That was the real estate tax. In almost every area of the country the taxes may have risen 30 to 100 per cent. But the income from the same property rose 100 to 300 per cent.

Later in learning your value formula, you will see that it makes no real difference that we use the formula on a proposed building where the rents are $110 per apartment and the tax rate $75 per thousand—or use it on a 1932 building where the same flat rented for $22 and the tax rate was $25.

Since we are talking about the type of real estate investment that *improves* with time, we must quickly and permanently reject any crepehangers who say it's too late now. I've heard it literally hundreds of times, usually followed by "you bought at the right time. There's no such good buys now." And that lets *that* cave-dweller out. While I was learning what not to buy, I learned something that was most significant at the same time. I learned not to be afraid. It was a most important change in my thinking. And it was quite natural under the circumstances. When the real estate investment field held many mysteries that I did not understand, I had the usual fear of the unknown, of the things that might hurt me. But with knowledge and experience comes confidence and fear fades. You, too, will soon experience the same thing. You will examine, evaluate, and decide yes or no. After a little experience, you will not be afraid.

In 1946 I heard about a property on University Road in our town. It consisted of a long row of three-decker Aunt Tobys, a few of which had basement apartments, making them four-family houses as to those units. The location was excellent. I could see, and YOU could have seen had you been there, that there was every indication that there would be a demand for those accommodations for many years to come. Even though they were owner-heated, they easily passed all tests, and I shortly bought them at a package price—$57,000. To do it, I had to take over an existing mortgage of some $42,000, give a second mortgage of $12,000 and pay $3,000 in cash.

The rents ranged about $50 per flat per month. The average occupancy for the tenants was about 15 years. The paint on the old New England style clapboards was peeling badly. The roofs leaked. There were a few more things that made up a picture of ownership by a "milker," one who took everything out and put nothing back unless forced to. I keep Uni, as we called it, for some 9 years. In that time, as I gave it better (and less hoggish) management, the income was used to put the buildings back into shape. Some matters required money. Others required little money, only some experience and common sense.

These were *not* depression times. Note the time element in this case. Try to put yourself into that year. In 1946, the war was just over. Prices had been rapidly rising. All my friends and "advisors" were certain that the reaction to the action of the past six years must surely come now. The war being over, things would drop fast. I cannot remember one of my friends who was optimistic. It was apparently universally accepted, without anyone rising to debate this "truism." "Things have been going up all through the war. Now, of course, they're going to go down—and quickly."

I studied the proposition again. The location was tops. Every other element of good investment was here. I announced that I was going to buy it. The reaction among my friends and business associates was much head-shaking. "Guess Bob has finally flipped. Gone too far. He'll break his neck sure, now. Ridin' for a big fall. You watch." Some even came to me imploring me to stop and think. "Look, Bob, the war is over! You've got to realize that all those prices have been rising and things have been booming. But now it's got to go *down!* It's time to pull in your horns. You'll lose all you've got. I'm telling you for your own good..."

But I refused to leave the standards I'd learned to accept. *I didn't care whether things went down or up.* I felt certain of two decisive things: (1) there would always be tenants who would buy my shelter in this location at a price I could sell at, and I would be making a fine profit. (2) nobody could build what these people wanted, where they wanted it, at a price to compare with mine. (That item of WHAT they wanted takes care of the item of government housing.) Remember, please, at that time I was *not* primarily seeking investments for resale. I wanted the income. I felt that I could have it in Uni. Let us see how the predictions of my friends and advisors worked out. Let us note how the element of *time* far from hurting us, helped us.

In contrast to the previous owner of Uni, who had been squeezing his entire living from the block, I was willing to plough back what was right. I wanted a good building in which lived reasonably contented tenants. It wasn't difficult.

In a short while, I had straightened out the minor needs, out of the income. Often ten dollars worth of plumbing repairs, neglected, can be the source of what seems a giant of annoyance in a building. And a neglected repair may cost the landlord one hundred times that sum in water bills. A few hours of a competent electrician straightened out other small but glaring needs. Besides, I installed some automatic electric clocks to turn the hall lights on and off, and the tenants were very grateful for the safety and comfort this little item brought them. They cost very little and did their job for decades.

Now I tackled the big items of the peeling paint. I'd learned that there was no permanent cure in painting a peeling house of this kind. So I had Sears come in (they do this type of contracting here as do many large sidewall companies), and they covered the outside walls with a high-quality *hard* asbestos shingle. Note this is not the cheap asphalt shingle used in many slums. These are solid, fireproof, heat insulators (insurance rates were lowered). They have a pastel coloring that is through and through the whole thickness, rather than a surface coloring that may be short lived. Now I had a good appearance and I would never have to paint again.

In the same contract I had new roofs installed and this pretty well absorbed the $12,000 that I'd cleared on the building thus far. But they looked so much better that the tenants were, with few grumbling exceptions, glad to pay a fair increase in rent. Note that these improvements were paid for out of the building rents themselves. In other words, the same tenants paid for the improvements as paid for the increased rents they brought. But they were more than happy to do it.

For some nine years I continued to derive a fine return from the buildings and, although we will dissect the transaction in greater detail later, it seems timely to point out how the dire predictions "that this is the wrong time" turned out. In 1955

I sold the block for $130,000. I took $15,000 down. I and my wife hold, as tenants by the entirety (and we'll explain this later) a mortgage for the remaining $115,000 for 30 years, which will pay us precisely $209,523.60 in interest and principal payments in that time. So we will have cleared from our original $3,000 investment:

Net earnings during the nine years we held it	$ 44,000.00
Down payment when we sold it	15,000.00
Total of payments in 30 year mortgage	209,523.60
Total	$268,523.60

Not bad for a $3,000 investment. And just bear in mind please, that this is not the best of my deals nor even the second best!

I was offered this property for $35,000 in 1932 and refused it, largely because it was heated and shabby. I arbitrarily rejected all such offers. At that time, I didn't know much about heating.

As I write this, we've been receiving our payments on the mortgage regularly. And the fellow who bought it from me has been paying steadily and promptly for some five years and is doing fine, thank you. As each year passes, our security grows better and better, and we're not worried. Even the collection of the payments is done for us automatically by my bank! We may be loafing on the Riviera and the money is being deposited in our account regularly and dependably. That's only *one* of our deals. There are better ones. And you can do the same thing, if you are not negative nor a cave dweller.

Let us choose a typical case among those whose fortunes I've guided. We will study one which has most of the action taking place in 1959, to confound those whose plaint is about this not being the right time.

About two years ago, Ed R. came to one of my classes in Real Estate Investment. He had a driving force behind him. He wanted to leave a killing job he held as an executive in a large firm. He was not negative. Just as most others have done, he asked me the standard question: "Bob, are you sure it's not too late? So many of my relatives and friends insist that the time for buying properties at good prices and with good returns is all over." I told him my standard answer and he decided to go ahead.

True, Ed R. had some money saved, and he was able to accelerate the process much more than one who starts with two to three thousand dollars. But his case still proves that it is *never* too late. As he acquired each three-decker or six-family Aunt Toby (and you will learn the methods of finding them in good time), he put it in order and started the flow of income. Ed did *not* drain income for living expenses. It was not long before the accumulated income showed a balance of $1,500 or so and he bought another. Today, as I write this, about two years after he started, Ed has some 82 tenants. The income grosses some $9,000 per month, and every tenant heats his own quarters. There are no janitors. I am not at liberty to disclose (he is my legal client) the exact net to Ed, but it is obvious what is being paid off on mortgages. Paid off, by whom? By the tenants! Sure, that's what we started out by saying—this is a wonderful business! And taxes bite into you but little, too. There are a few other typical and significant facts I should mention about Ed's enterprise.

... Bulletin: he has quit his job and is moving up to the final step as described in Chapter 25. His income is secure, far more secure than it ever could be on the job. If he should be sick, for instance, the income continues unbroken.

Then, as you can see, the net cash in hand leaves him in a position to take advantage of any new buys that come along— out of his profits. That's what may be termed the pleasantest kind of pyramiding. Because, let me emphasize this, Ed has almost *never* bought a building in which he was required to invest much more than $3,000. In almost every case, the bank loaned some 80 per cent of the purchase price, the seller took back a second mortgage for perhaps 10 per cent and Ed put the remaining 10 per cent down in cash. In a few more years the second mortgages will be paid off and the amount cleared each month will rise substantially.

There are a few other sidelights that are typical in these cases, and they have emerged in Ed's case too.

Ed has become *known* as a buyer of these properties. Every real estate man and woman in the area has an eagle eye out for these properties to make commissions by selling them to Ed. He has become *the* buyer of three-deckers in the entire area. Owners and even banks seek him out when they have one for sale. Some brokers *solicit* owners of three-deckers to sell, and if they get assent, contact Ed. A few weeks ago, I attended a passing of title on some more of his acquisitions. He had just been asked by a bank to take over a neglected three-decker with a store in the first floor and three apartments above—price $10,000. He was "out of breath" with the pace of his absorption and his rise, and asked my advice. The location? Good. Value formula shows it to be a good buy? "Yes," I snapped, "buy it."

Then there are the banks. Of course, the various bankers in the area meet and exchange news of their business. They have come to rate Ed as tops. He puts and keeps the property in shape. That is good security and a civic blessing too. He pays his bills promptly. That builds fine financial rating, and suggests honest, non-greedy and intelligent management.

The banks also are thoroughly conscious of another point. If they lend money to a buyer of a one-family single house, the payment to the bank is comparatively hanging by a thread. The *entire* payment must come from one wage-earner's pay envelope. And that wage-earner can encounter many things that will interrupt the payments. He may become ill, lose his job, take up gambling, split with his wife, or have a need for heavy medical expense for a sick child. That puts the bank in an unenviable position if it insists on payment in spite of the "temporary setback" the borrower is suffering.

But in the case of loaning money on a three-decker, there are at least *three* pay envelopes involved, and that much more security. What's more, of these three, none is carrying the huge burden of maintaining a single house. Even should one paycheck cease for a time, the others easily carry the bank obligation, and the bank achieves precisely what it wants, payment with regularity and dependability.

We could not leave the Ed R. case even for the moment without mentioning another favorable condition that has become established in his community. The *tenants* have come to know, in this short time, that Ed is fair. He keeps his buildings in reasonable shape. It is getting to be *the* desirable thing among the workingmen tenants who have been considering a change, to "try to get one of Ed's flats."

Yes, success breeds success. Supply-houses unload outdated stocks of wallpaper and paint on Ed. He gives it to the tenants to apply, by their own efforts, or at their own expense. The same with electric light fixtures. Where for 50 years there hung an ugly cord or chain in the middle of a bedroom or dining room, now glows a beautiful modern light fixture. The life of each fixture is about 50 years or more. Cost? In the vicinity of $1.75 each. Ed is constantly solicited to buy floor coverings, sinks and other things that cost little, once installed are permanent, and no wonder his tenants are happy!

Ed's method in getting started was the one I teach regularly, simplicity itself, and we will set it forth here soon, but first another case which I must preface with the remark that this is NOT typical. It is probably the most outstanding single real estate transaction with which I have had experience or contact. It is not in itself large by comparison. It contains, however, some of the most outstanding evidence of the truth of my statement that *there is still plenty of room* so that it deserves recounting here.

11

ARE THERE STILL GOOD BUYS?

Some years ago, a young housewife came to my classes to learn real estate. She had five small children. Her husband worked at a government plant as an executive. Recently her father had died, leaving her and her brother some $3,000 each.

Dorothea wanted to supplement the family income and her brother had agreed with her that they would learn real estate, try to enter the field with a little brokerage, and as time developed, start to invest their nest egg in some real estate as partners. Dorothea's husband agreed to baby-sit while she attended evening classes. The brother took my course at home on records.

When they had finished their training, Dorothea found time to practice a little real estate brokerage and to put into operation the methods you will learn here for finding income property of the Aunt Toby type. Dorothea lived in a very small town, but the adjoining cities of Framingham and Natick, Massachusetts, are near Dorothea's home and she recognized that the presence of large segments of workingmen in these cities offered her the best opportunity for development of her plans for that reason. There is a General Motors assembly plant in Framingham, employing thousands. Nearby a Ford plant gives a livelihood to thousands more—all on a permanent basis. A brewery, a large government installation, a huge stationery supply plant of many generations history, and other commercial enterprises in the area promise that this will always be a good spot for the type of rentals we offer.

As Dorothea started to spread her message in brokerage and as a prospective buyer of Aunt Tobys the word got around. You will learn just how to get started too—in clear, simple, unmistakable instructions. These instructions have *never* failed yet! That leads me to a point that I should mention here. Dorothea was not an outstanding girl. She was a normal happy wife and mother. If there were any distinguishing characteristics about her they were simply these.

She would apply herself. She would try to do fully, thoroughly, what she undertook. She did her lessons in my class that way. She *found* time, unlike many others, to do them well and have them ready on time. I noted her sincerity, of course, and I was optimistic, but never dreamed she was slated to go as far or as fast as the future proved.

She was never negative. She had made up her mind to learn how and to move ahead in the light of her knowledge. She thought positively. She was *going* to do it. It was as simple as that. She was resolved to banish fear and doubt. Perhaps she felt that she would never starve anyway, since she would be provided for as a wife by her dependable husband, even if she lost her (and her brother's) nest-egg. This may have given her courage beyond the norm, but I doubt it. In this regard many other students simply earned their starter-investment by commissions on sales of real estate and risked that. I think they were, on the average, no different in their attitudes, depending on the individual.

Dorothea had some $6,000 to play with, and full authority to go ahead and invest it. Brother consulted with her but always agreed to her proposals.

A few months after she graduated, I officiated at the passing of the deed in which Dorothea acquired her first Aunt Toby. She invested about $1300 in cash. She continued her search for more of them, using the methods I will set out here. A few more months and she had located a duplex Toby. Six families.

All the Tests proved positives and the Value Formula said—
"*Offer the owner so much*" (as in the previous one)—and under
the following terms. She did. Some of the $1500 that she put
down on No. 2 was money milked from No. 1. Then one day she
called me about No. 3.

The facts were so intriguing that I went personally to inspect it for hidden flaws. Since it was perhaps the most outstanding example of my experience, it deserves explicit detail
here. The details in No. 3 are so brilliantly and unimpeachably
proof of the truism that there still *is* plenty of room, that I ask
you to put your mind into certain orbits before approaching
the facts.

Put yourself in 1946. Imagine that you have just talked over
the advisability of buying a certain property. You've just explained that all the figures and facts prove it is a good move.
Your friend shakes his head and figuratively strokes his beard.
You are told, "Stay out of it. You're heading for trouble. Things
are bound to go down—but *down*. They've been rising steadily
for six years. For every action there must be a reaction. All the
good buys were bought up in the depression by the smart ones.
Now it's too late. And mind you, why do you think he wants
to sell it? If it was any good, he'd keep it, not sell it. No, better
keep your money. You'd lose your shirt." Now, in the light of
that sage advice (which is exactly what I received), think of
what happened with the Uni property. Think what I would
have missed if I had listened to the good-intentioned advice of
my well-meaning friends. The psychological implications in
this advice, as a trained psychologist would analyze it, are
devious and mysterious. But any layman can see here that the
advisor wants: (1) to appear very wise; (2) to appear superior
in his judgment to you; (3) to justify his own stagnation in
mediocrity and secretly (although perhaps he does not realize
it) to prevent you from moving up and thus spotlighting and
proving HIS failure to move ahead.

Now put yourself into 1948. I was contemplating the Collonades block. The details of this one will be set forth in a later
chapter, but imagine that you have talked *this* one over with

another sage. The words and music are still the same. But you remember what happened in the Uni property? This one turned out even better, much better!

Now flash yourself through 1952, for much the same scene, and pause a moment at 1955. In that year, I sold Len and Lois G. a package of Aunt Tobys soon after they had graduated from my course. They, too, consulted their "best friend and advisor." Need I say that the advice was much the same? But they bought them. As I write this, I pause to phone the G's. Are they happy? Deliriously! Of course, I could go on and on with this, but you get my point.

As you place yourself in each of these years, and see that the pattern never changes, you should now be able to see the crepehanger in the light of these experiences. He or his counterpart is saying almost the same words at this moment to someone. In most cases he succeeds in scaring him and he settles back in his rut, side by side with the crepehanger, and ten, twenty and thirty years from today, they are just where they were, but both of them bitter. Now, with this background for your thinking, let us see what happened with Dorothea's No. 3.

She and I went to look over No. 3. It was a little off the pattern of the usual Aunt Tobys, but interesting. It consisted of a row of eight single houses in Philadelphia style, that is, wall to wall. Each had two stories, attics and basements. Some had their toilets in their cellars. Some had been partially modernized. The exterior had been covered with the cheap, ugly asphalt siding material that is often sold by high-pressure home-improvement salesmen. The present owner had neglected everything except collection of rent. Of course, we should consider first, the thing of first importance—Location.

The property was on Avenue N, some five minutes' walk from the center, schools and shopping. It was in a very desirable residential neighborhood consisting largely of single homes which were nicely maintained by their owners. It was a nice place to live, and anyone could see that the rentability (or saleability) would benefit by excellent location. As a matter of interest, we later learned that this property was considered the

eyesore and ugly duckling of the otherwise good neighborhood
and the homeowners in the area hoped and prayed it would be
demolished.

In the first and most vital test, No. 3 passed with flying colors.
We could feel certain that in this city and in this location, we
would have no difficulty getting tenants at the rents we contemplated charging. Now a little about the history of the property.

A former owner had sadly neglected the place to a point
where it was abandoned to the bank for the balance on a small
mortgage. A prominent realty broker and investor, in fact
the most prominent real estate broker in the area, one Mr. H.,
had obligingly taken it off the bank's hands at this low figure.
Mark you, Mr. H. was no novice. He really knew real estate
after some forty years of successful practice in the same city.
Now, Mr. H. was winding up his affairs and moving to Florida
permanently and was disposing of his holdings. Of course, such
a reason usually causes lifted eyebrows, but we rarely attach
ANY importance to the reason for selling anyway. If we were
to rely on this, we would have a poor yardstick indeed for determining which properties to buy and which to refuse. Just
curious, that's all.

Mr. H. had offered the parcel to a dealer, a friend of mine, a
Mr. T. who bought and sold low-priced properties. Mr. T.
maintained a crew of repairmen to do the remodeling. He had
sent out his buyer-agent and when Mr. H. named his price for
the eight houses, the agent had promptly (and automatically)
offered him some 25 per cent less. As was the agent's custom,
he went away and waited for the seller to come to terms.

Some time passed. When Mr. H. saw Dorothea's ad (that
you will use as your prime means of acquiring Aunt Tobys), he
called her and asked her to look them over. They weren't
exactly the thing she had been advertising for, but they certainly passed all three of our tests with flying colors.

Their location was, for our purposes, and using the yardstick
of the rent expected, excellent. Put in simple terms, and at the
risk of seeming repetitious, when you drove up the street, and

looked around, you would instantly notice that this location for
that rent was fine!

The rents that the owner was getting were in the same degree of neglect as the buildings themselves. Some old tenants
were occupying an eight-room house, albeit with poor facilities
and accommodations, for $26 per month! In 1958! To apply a
reasonable rate was simple. Would $75-per-month tenants buy
these shelters in this location readily? The answer was obvious.
Of course. So it was OK as to test No. 2—modest rents.

The third test, that of heat, was OK here too. Therefore, it
was time to apply the Value Formula that you will learn in a
later chapter. That recommended a purchase price that was
drastically out of line with the price the seller wanted. And it
was out of line in reverse relation to the usual. The Value
Formula said it was worth more than twice what the owner
wanted! And that's what made the thing suspicious.

So I went over to examine it. In those days, Dorothea would
often ask me to look over a property and check her figures.
Later she felt secure in relying on her own observations and
judgments, especially when she saw how little I really con-
tributed to what she already knew, having carefully studied
what you will learn here.

I have deliberately refrained from mentioning the specific
prices in the history of this parcel. I wanted you to view the
thing without that distraction. Now that you have been filled
in on the history to thus orient you with the proposition, it
seems the right time to set out the figures. I do not know what
Mr. H. bought (or took it over) for. I would hazard a guess
based upon my examination of the previous deeds and the
mortgage picture in the title search, that he took it over for
the mortgage balance that was owed the bank at the time—
perhaps $13,000. In the time he owned it he gradually reduced
this balance to some $11,000. He offered it to the buyer-agent
for $16,000 and received a counter-offer of about $12,000 which
he refused.

It is interesting to note at this point the policy of the buyer-
agent. He had no Value Formula. He went by guess-and-by-

God. If he thought a property could be fixed up by his company
and sold for a good profit, he would try to buy it. But he had
been spoiled. By the very nature of the parcels that he had been
buying, he was put in the driver's seat as to price. He had
been able to virtually name his own price. And still he had been
able for years to buy properties for his company to the tune of
some ten a week! That was and is due to the unique market
conditions that obtain as to neglected property. In its proper
order, we will elaborate on this condition. But there was one
policy that the buyer-agent never deviated from. He would
never pay the price the seller wanted. Yes, even if the seller
asked one-half or one-quarter the worth of the property; even if
it was *obviously* a great bargain, he would offer less, much less.
Then he would wait. In most cases he got it for his price.

But he missed out on many, many good buys, simply because
he pursued this policy. He knew no Value Formula. If he had
known one, he could quickly have figured out an exact price
that the property was worth. Then he would have compared
this with the asking price. If, as often was the case, the seller
was asking much less, he would have made it his business not
to let the property slip out of his hands, and many a profitable
investment for his company was lost to them because of this
policy, or lack of it.

When I examined the property and its surroundings with
Dorothea, I asked her for the fourth or fifth time this question: "Are you sure there's no mistake or misunderstanding? He
wants $17,000 for *ALL eight houses?*"

"Yes, I checked it carefully after we talked on the phone
and you raised the point. That's what Mr. H. wants. *For all
eight.*"

I replied, "I can't believe it. I would find it hard enough to
believe the price you mention if the property was offered by
someone who didn't know its worth. If the seller was perhaps
some heir who had just inherited it and wanted no part of it—
wanted to dump it at once for any price. But you tell me it is
owned by Mr. H.! He is a seasoned veteran in this business
and in this town. It can't be true."

But Dorothea was certain. And, knowing her, I felt that she had the facts correctly. So I suggested that we go straightway to the office of Mr. H. and see if we could close a deal. We sat down with Mr. H. and after some preliminary talk, offered him $14,000. We finally settled on $14,500 as the price. We signed a contract, which we call simply an Agreement. In various parts of the country this is often called an *agreement of purchase and sale,* or Bond for a Deed. The Agreement required Dorothea to buy at $14,500 in one of two ways. Mr. H. was to try to place a new mortgage for $13,000 and she would put $1,500 down. There was another proviso to make sure the sale did not fall through. If Mr. H. failed to find us a lender for a new first mortgage, it was agreed that Dorothea would take over and assume the old first mortgage of $11,000, give Mr. H. a second mortgage for $2,000, and the $1,500 balance in cash.

Mr. H. probably never knew it, but when we sat down to dicker on this sale, we were determined not to leave until we had him signed up. As soon as the agreement was signed, I breathed easier. This type of contract is one of the most binding and inescapable in legal jurisprudence.

In due course, Mr. H. applied to several banks for the new mortgage for $13,000, blanketing all eight houses under the one mortgage. The various appraisers and security committees from the banks inspected the property and all turned it down. This will be of great significance to us later when we learn how to buy and finance Aunt Tobys. The very difficulty that Mr. H. had in trying to place a comparatively puny mortgage on shabby property is often the very reason that we can buy them at our own price. The seller has become discouraged as buyer after buyer fails to obtain financing for the sale, and the seller then will accept our terms. Yes, it is true. Even the bank's "experts" can't see what you will see in these money-makers.

Accordingly, Dorothea bought the property by assuming the old $11,000 mortgage and gave a new second mortgage for $2,000 and $1,500 in cash. Now she turned her attention to cleaning it up and putting it on a paying basis.

There were some glaring needs in improvement, of course, but the net income left a good margin for that. It could easily be paid for out of the profit from the rents. Let us look at the *immediate* future of No. 3.

Within a short time, after some refurbishing of the exterior appearance, we could easily expect rentals averaging $75 per month per house, with the tenants heating themselves. This meant a gross income of eight times $75 = $600 per month or $7,200 per year. Thus:

Gross annual income $7,200
Expenses (and this means *true* expenses, excluding
        principal payments, which are not.)

Taxes	$600	
Interest on mortgages 5% on $13,000	650	
Water	200	
Insurance	322	
Maintenance	300	
Total true expenses		$2,072

Balance after deducting expenses from income on
   an investment of $1,500! $5,128 per yr.

Now there were some "catches" in this proposition still to be considered.

First, the matter of the repairs needed to put the property into decent shape to *earn* the $75 per month per house, as rent. As you can see from the above statement of income and expenses, the rents themselves would leave enough money clear in hand each month so that the money for these repairs would quickly accumulate without any contribution from Dorothea. As each month passed and she noted the balance in hand, she cleaned up the next repair on her list. The ugly sidewall covering could wait, but the trim was neatly painted a dark green. The rotted front wooden steps to each house were replaced with concrete for permanent service.

Each tenant was forbidden to park his car on his front yard. There was plenty of room on the land in the rear of the buildings. The front yards were fenced with inexpensive iron pipe and the tenants were given flower and grass seeds. Once they were started, some put up window boxes of flowers, too. Very soon the building was no longer an eyesore. And the desirability to tenants grew with every move. Some plumbing had to be done and as soon as sufficient money accumulated, a few modern baths and kitchens were installed. It is not surprising in view of this, that there was soon a long waiting list of tenants.

Now in any true picture of the financial situation of a building, we must take into consideration that there are some items which, although they do not properly classify as expenses, nevertheless require us to pay out money from our net income. Since we are concerned here primarily with the methods you will use for pyramiding, this means we should spell out every item for which you will have to pay out money. Otherwise you would not have a true and really workable picture of what you would have left in hand for re-investment. So let us take the true profit shown above and substract from it the other items, cash and "paperwise" that we will have to pay out, so that we will see the final and true-to-life figure that we will work with. Here is how that figures:

True profit per year as above		$5,128
Further losses and payouts not usually classified as expenses:		
Principal payments on first mortgage average during first five years	$380	
Principal payments on 2nd mortgage	175	
Rental loss during vacancy periods and repairs (this figure reduces to a nominal tiny amount after the building is going along)	300	
Interest on buyer's investment money:		
Dorothea would now lose interest on her $1,500	60	
Total other payouts and expenses	$915	915
Leaving a balance in hand per year, of		$4,213

But—

We must remember that in addition to this sum, Dorothea

was becoming enriched each year by $555 which was being paid off on her mortgages by the tenants. If you think this is a pretty nice little deal, read on, and hold on to your hat. I had bigger and better plans for Dorothea on No. 3.

As soon as she had "caught her breath" here was the next step I proposed. Now remember, I told you in the beginning of this chapter that this purchase was outstanding and *not* routine. It was a juicier deal than the others. But it does demonstrate several points.

I advised Dorothea *not* to lease the houses. She should rent them from month to month with the written proviso that she could show them at any time to repairmen or to prospective purchasers, and each tenant agreed to vacate within a reasonable time if the building were sold. Then we would *sell them off* individually to single purchasers. After they had been cleaned up we could easily get $12,000 each if we offered attractive terms. Perhaps $500 down on each house, providing the buyer had a background of good credit and was a steady type. This would leave her a mortgage to hold for perhaps 25 years. Her only bother from then on would be to collect the payments each month, and even that would be handled for her at nominal charge by her bank. The buyer would receive a notice each month from the bank and he would make his payment to the bank and it would be deposited to her account. In calculating the figures, I will leave out the deposits that the buyer would make each month to accumulate for payment of the annual tax bill. Since that is not money which Dorothea would really own, but would only hold in escrow, we should not concern ourselves with it. We will address ourselves to the actual payments on mortgages. Let us see how she will stand.

When she sells all eight houses she will have received for her $1,500 investment:

Net income while she held them (approximate)	$ 8,000
Down payments on sale of eight at $500 each	4,000
Leaving her in hand after she sold all	$12,000

This will permit her to invest this $12,000 for further gain. Thus she would now be receiving:

Interest on the $12,000 let us say, at 4%, minimally, $ 480 per year

Interest and principal payments on eight mortgages, each at 6% on 25 year basis—total
$92,000.00, payments total $7,114.56 per year $7,114.56

giving her a total annual income of $7,594.56

This income would be free of attention, management, re-pairs, etc. That figures out to an income of $136.80 per week for 25 years—*plus* the fact she would have $12,000 available for further investments—and pyramiding! Let us note how much she would take out of the deal in all in the 25 years. Here is the exact amount—$177,864. On a $1,500 investment! All she needed was the *know-how* you will have after reading and digesting this book.

Do you think this a fine deal? Just wait! We have *better* ones to study. But let us hope that by this time you have banished from your mind all vestiges of negativeness, particularly as to that oldie, "there just aren't any more good buys around." And you can test yourself at this point, if you are interested. That is, you can now find out for yourself whether you ARE inclined to be negative. I have set a trap for you above. I deliberately led you into a situation where, if you are the slightest bit negative it would show up. Here is how you can test yourself.

When I gave you the figures in the Dorothea matter, and they are *true* figures, did you find yourself worrying about how much income taxes you would have to pay if *you* were making this money? If so, you are inclined to be negative. Your mind needs a determined purging of this attitude. If you did not think of income taxes as you read the figures you are indeed a good bet to succeed in this enterprise. How about taxes? Easy. There is very little income tax to be paid on our type of earning. We have Capital Gain benefits, depreciation allowances and many other special privileges accorded *only* to real estate investors. Don't concern yourself about it. I will explain exactly how to arrange your program to pay very little tax. And, besides, you should never mind taxes. My attitude is, I'm darn glad to make it and pay my taxes. I hope it will be yours. That is the attitude of a *positive* thinker.

Let us sew up the Dorothea story. Here are the points that it proves:

There are, and undoubtedly will be, plenty of good buys left. Some are just good. Others are excellent. Occasionally, one is fantastic, as in Dorothea's case. But, if you know what to do and what NOT to do, you will find a fertile field for decades to come. Unless, of course, too many buy my book and follow its methods. But I believe negativity will keep that in check.

The most sagacious, experienced, shrewd owners often sell you the best buys. Wait until I explain the Freeman deal, which I bought from a real sharpshooter. But he didn't know the Value Formula. I did. There's a fine income picture in *holding* the property, if you know how and what to buy—there's a pretty nice picture in *selling* it if you know how.

You can usually make your start with very little capital. Of the last one hundred properties my students have bought in the past two years, I only know of four where they put more than $3,000 down. All the others required less. You can get your capital out very quickly and buy another. Then *two, four,* then *eight.* That is real pyramiding. It is only possible if you buy real estate and if you know how.

Our special benefits in the Real Estate Field permit us to get rich as in no other field.

12

HOW TO FIND THE GOOD BUYS

Now that we have disposed of WHAT to buy and how to double check its features and suitability, you know what to look for when you see a property. We next undertake the subject of how to find them. It is quite simple and easy. There are three main methods.

METHOD NO. 1

By far the most productive method, you will find, is persistent advertising. Besides watching the ads of properties for sale, you should place a small ad, using no display or large type. This is an important rule. When a buyer uses large ads or ads that have too much "anxiousness and push" about them, or even when they are written too professionally, they lose their effectiveness. The average owner of an Aunt Toby does not want to deal with professionals. The reasons are obvious. The owner is in the same category in this regard as the fellow who sells a used car. He is convinced that if he sells it to a dealer he will get a price far below the price he could have obtained if he had sold it to a "private party." Further, it offends his pride. Except for those rare cases where a seller is in a desperate position and must sell at once, and for any price, he will shy away from people who, he suspects, are real estate dealers. That is, dealers why buy properties at distress prices and sell them for full market value.

That is why a large ad, or one which promises "fast action" or "pay top price" or "cash waiting" or "quick action" is usually unproductive. The seller is made to feel as if he is selling to a pawn-broker or to a junkdealer—and for a price accordingly.

The ads should be placed in your local newspaper, and once begun, changed as to wording from time to time. But resolve to persist. Stick with it or don't begin it. Remember you are buying what you will have to "live with" for a long time. It is you who are holding out your hand with the money. That will bring many to your door in time. Some of these will have good properties to offer, others, junk. You are not in any hurry. That, too, is a potent factor on your side. So run these ads about once or twice a week for a year or so as a starter. They should go into a classification, if available, of Real Estate Wanted. If there is no such classification readily available in your paper, ask the advertising manager to start one. Often the ad-taker just does not know that this classification is available, so before you accept a substitute, press firmly for a final word from the Advertising Manager on this point. If there is no such classification obtainable, use the classification of Real Estate. And here's a little off-beat hint. Once in a while, run the ad on the front page of the paper. It is much more expensive but often catches the eye of the reader better than one tucked away in the classified section. Here are the ads that have brought success to every one of my students who have been reasonably persistent.

---

3 or 6-family wanted. Private buyer. (Your
phone no.)

Wanted. 3 family or 6-family in decent (or
"good") location. I am not a dealer. (Your
phone no.)

Small Rental Building Wanted. Private
Buyer. 3 or more family. (Phone no.)

Wanted: 3 or 6 family. Condition not important but must have good location. I am not buying as a dealer or a broker. (Phone no.)

Property In Good Location Wanted By Private Buyer. Condition not important. Prefer unheated. 3 or 6 family. (Phone no.)

If you are only at home to receive calls in the evenings, you should add the word "evenings"after the phone number.

Although as we have seen above, the words "quick action" are not good for general use, you will often get good results by varying your ad with an occasional one that emphasizes your willingness and ability to close the deal without delay.

This is especially true in those cases where an owner who WANTS to get rid of the property is fed up with deal after deal falling through for one reason or another. He has been told repeatedly by his broker that the property is "sold." Each time he has taken it off the market, and waited for the slow action of lender banks as the prospective buyer applies to one after the other for the mortgage loan. Then, after weeks and sometimes months of delay, the sale falls through and he is back where he started.

He is in the mood now to close a deal on almost any terms that *will* finish the business. When we discuss your unique methods of arranging financing on purchases, it will be apparent that if he is amenable enough, you can do what the others failed to do. You can take it off his hands and give him what he wants—an end to it.

In several of the purchases I have made, I distinctly recall how heavily this issue weighed in getting the deal consummated. When Mr. L. came to my office with the figures on No. 16, he set a price of $35,000. I had seen the building and made up my mind long since that I wanted it. It consisted of eleven, four-room suites. Heat was supplied by the owner, but not hot water nor janitor service.

After doing the Value Formula, I offered $25,000. He made

as if to leave. I let him. Then he came back to his chair and offered to sell at $30,000. I held firm. He didn't know it, but he wasn't going to get out of the office (that is, not ALL the way out), without closing a deal. I insisted that $25,000 was my limit. The remark he made then will give you a hint as to the importance and usefulness of the wish on the part of the seller to make an end to it. He said, "Bob, what do you mean by you will 'give me $25,000?' Not that I'd sell it for that, but do you mean that you *will* buy it for that or do you mean that *if* you can get a given amount of mortgage loan, then only, will you buy?"

I replied that if he accepted the offer, I would give him $1,000 then and there and we would sign an agreement, and the remaining $24,000 when we passed papers. No escapes. No if's nor but's. That clinched it. I was giving him what he wanted badly—a finish to the whole matter.

I had previously approached the local bank about a mortgage. When I told the mortgage officer I would probably be buying No. 16, he replied, "Oh, that one again!" Then I knew that other prospective buyers had previously been in to see him and had shopped around for financing without success. The amount they had been offered on mortgage by the banks had been so low that they would have been required to invest twelve or fifteen thousand dollars of their own cash, which took the deal out of their reach.

The mortgage officer told me that he would loan $19,000 to me which meant that my total investment would be $6000 to complete the purchase.

As for Mr. L., he wanted an end to the thing—now. I offered him just that, albeit at a not-too-attractive price. But by now, the desire for a consummation was having a strong effect on the hope for a big selling price. He was fed up with the "almost" sales. I offered him a deal that was flat, final, and without an escape clause. Thus it transpired that the element of *time* had tipped the scales for me. In later transactions, the Waban and Sharon purchases, the same inducement and motivation were the deciding factors in getting the deal closed.

For this reason, I developed an ad in addition to the others, which gives assurance to those owners who are discouraged by repeated failures of deals. In the same light, I offer what they seek to those sellers to whom the most important thing is immediacy of action. Here is the ad:

3-6 family owner. If you wish to sell at a fair price without delay I can arrange to close the deal COMPLETELY in 3 days. (Phone no.)

---

or;

Will buy in 3 days. Want 3 or 6-family at fair price. Can complete entire transaction in 3 days. (Phone no.)

To back up this offer, you will need to make arrangements with a lawyer who understands your financing methods and who will make it his business to do the title and paper work accordingly. As a lawyer, I have found that this is perfectly practical. Of course not ALL your deals will be the three-day type, but you will have no difficulty in locating a competent lawyer in your city who will be glad to have all your business, the quickies, with the leisurely deals.

In no case should you ever use a box number ad, or blind ad. If you have a choice of which phone number to advertise, always choose the one that is not a toll call, of course. In some areas there is an extra charge for calls to phones in city centers.

METHOD NO. 2

This method should never be begun until at least a month of advertising. Since Method No. 2 uses the realty brokers in your area, there will always be a commission involved in any properties you buy through them. Usually there are several buildings in your area that have been on the market for some time, when you enter the field. The owners of these may well see your ad and call you direct, and you thus save 5 per cent or more of the price. That is why it is best to give the direct ads a

chance for a month or so before starting to use Method No. 2.
If you went to the brokers at once, you might well be offered
a property that, through your ad, would have been brought to
your attention by the owner direct, and thus save you $700 to
$1000. So give the ads a reasonable chance first. Then start
Method No. 2. In Method No. 2, we phone or write all the
realty brokers in the area. You will find them in the yellow
pages of your phone book.

When you call them, do *not* tell them that you require that
the buildings pass our three tests, with the exception of that of
location. It is well to prevent waste of time looking at buildings
that are in bad locations, but as to the other requirements,
self-heat, and modest rents, hold the door open and be willing
to look at a property even if the landlord supplies heat. Our
country is so varied in climates, customs and conditions that
in many areas you must buy what we call "heated property" or
none. Further, you will be protected against making a bad buy
by your application of the Value Formula. And these buildings,
although they bring with them myriad headaches that we do
not endure with unheated property, are often very profitable.

Also, as to the rule requiring that the rents be modest, we
must keep an open mind. As I write this book here in New
England, I can say that in 1973 a $125 per month rent is a mod-
est one. But there are so many variants in different parts of the
country that I must ask you not to pin this down as an arbi-
trary rule. Again, your Value Formula will protect you against
a poor buy, but you will be able to judge whether there is and
probably will be, a good future demand for these apartments at
these rents. Then you will apply our tests as to location and
the Value Formula. If it passes these tests, you will go into the
matter of financing and then make your offer.

METHOD NO. 3

This method involves several simple means of spreading the
word to the various areas where your properties might be. A
phone call or note to the mortgage officer of the various banks

in your area will alert them to the fact that you are a prospective buyer of this type of property. They often have some that have been foreclosed, or, in some cases, the bank is trustee-manager of some of them for an estate. It does no harm in any case to tell them you are in the market.

Then there's the tour-and-look way. You should drive around, up one street and down the other. A "for sale" sign on a building will tell you it is on the market. Often you will see an Aunt Toby in a good neighborhood, but in neglected condition. Just jot down the number. Then ask a tenant to tell you who owns the building. If you cannot get the information from the tenants, a call to the assessor, or the tax collector will usually elicit the information. If both of those are blind alleys, you will find that there is an address at the water department where the bills are sent. These means have never failed me in finding the owner for a direct deal.

When you reach the owner, ask him if he is interested in selling. If not, leave your name and address. If yes is the answer, you now get the facts and figures and you are making a start.

ANSWERING CALLS

It is important that we take a moment here to learn just how to answer calls that these methods bring to you. If you should receive a call from an owner who is suspicious that you are really a dealer in properties, or a broker looking for listings, and that you are trying to give the false impression that you are a buyer, you should be a little patient with him. It pays. Don't forget that he is not to be blamed for being suspicious. He may have answered many ads already. Some of them proclaimed that the advertiser wanted to buy property, but it soon developed that, "Well, that's not exactly what *I'm* looking for, but I have a client who would be interested. I also sell properties for a commission. Why don't you *list* it with me?" Just a broker looking for listings with bait advertising.

Besides, he has probably run up against the scavengers who are always advertising their willingness to buy, but who, upon examination, turn out to be dealers who only want to buy at distress prices, taking advantage of the folks who are hard pressed to sell. So he may cross-examine you when he calls you. Don't let it throw you or stifle your sense of humor. Take the attitude that he has every right to ask all the questions he wishes and get all the frank answers he wants *before* disclosing his deal. I have found that this technique pays off.

If you have planted the seeds as described above, you will find results sprouting soon. Not only that, but all my experience, and it's a mighty *broad* experience, in many areas and in various times and circumstances, has shown that you WILL get results, all you want!

Some readers will find this question popping up in their minds, "Shall I ask him why he's selling?" It matters very little If you're curious, go ahead and ask him. As a practical matter we place no weight on his answer. Our buying methods completely eliminate all reliance on his reasons. He might have the best reasons in the world for selling. He might be able to invent a glorious lie. It's all the same to us. We test, decide, and that's it.

Now that we have discussed what to buy and how to find them, we are ready to learn how to figure out what the property is worth. We call it the Value Formula.

13

THE IMPORTANCE AND USES OF
THE VALUE FORMULA

Now we must get down to figures. Assuming
that the property has passed your three tests of eligibility, and
you feel that it is a good property for your purposes, we now
learn what you should pay for it. There is no necessity to emphasize the importance of this process. Even if you never read
this book, you would certainly know that if you pay too much
for a property, you are entering a deal in which you can make
little or no profit. Conversely, you *should be ready to pay a
certain price!* In no other way can you spot the good buys. That
means the property for which the owner wants less (and sometimes FAR less) than it is worth. Obviously you proceed to
buy these with a minimum of dickering and delay. And, mark
you, there WILL be such buys from time to time.

The importance of a thorough understanding of the Value
Formula cannot be exaggerated. It is as much your means of
measurement as if you were a buyer of yard goods and were
setting out to buy some cloth. Would you let it be measured off
by guesswork? In the same light, a property is worth a certain
amount. And when you say it is worth that much you are saying
many more things, between the lines.

You are saying that if a buyer pays the Value Formula

71

amount for it, he can safely depend upon it that he will make a fine return on his investment.

You are saying that at this price, with a fair finance plan arranged, he will have a nice net profit in hand each year that will give him back his investment in a comparatively short time.

You are saying that if he has any of the usual setbacks, he will not be seriously hurt. That means if, after a time, a new roof is required, there will be a fat accumulation of profits out of which to pay for it.

The use of the Value Formula becomes even more important when we consider that it will establish a price. That price will be the one which you will feel for years in the payments that you will saddle yourself with for twenty or twenty-five years.

Then there is the matter of confidence. You will have a sense of sureness that you know what you are doing. If the Formula says—"Give him $18,000" (with a leeway of 5% either way) you *know* that when you refuse to pay him $19,000, you are making no mistake, even if you like the building and want it. You know that you are doing the right thing, and you reiterate the offer and withdraw and wait. Your conscience need feel no qualms. You've made no mistake.

THE USES OF THE VALUE FORMULA

There are four major uses of the Value Formula. The first use will often be of help to you. In most sales, there is the traditional Alphonse-and-Gaston wrangle and haggle about price, with each side repeating again and again that it is worth so much, only to have the other side repeat that it is worth SO much. And you get nowhere. Both sides are expressing *opinions*. And opinions, of themselves, are worth little, unless substantiated by some evidence. The Value Formula gives you that evidence. You have an authoritative form with which you can sit down with an owner and demonstrate the true market value of the property—by the *printed word*. That often carries great weight. It gives you something more than just your opinion against the seller's. Often I have seen it convince the seller.

The second (and third) use of the Value Formula apply only to the real estate brokers. If you are a broker, interested only in making a commission, you will use the formula to convince buyers that the property is worth what the seller wants. Again, the printed authority will help you when you need something more than your opinion against the buyer's. With the Value Formula, you can demonstrate and prove authoritatively the market value of the building. In this regard, as brokers, you will use the Formula to help convince sellers, too, that they are asking too much, thus getting them to offer the property for a reasonable figure so that you can more easily sell it and make your commission.

The third use of the Formula is for making official appraisals. Brokers and appraisers are often called upon to make an appraisal for an estate, for a bank, for a tax assessment purpose, and for many other requirements. You will have a formalized, substantiated, neat and orderly method of arriving at an exact figure. Also, when you are up on the witness stand being cross-examined by the attorney for the taxpayer, you will be sure of yourself. He demands, "This figure you have given in your appraisal is just your opinion, is it not?"

You answer quietly, "No, it is not."

Usually you will get as the next question, "Then what is it?"

You reply, "It is an exact appraisal, fully and properly made."

Now, (and I've never seen it fail) he comes back with, "Just how did you arrive at this figure?"

That question is what ruins his case. Your answer is going to take between fifteen minutes and one hour, but he, having asked it, must listen (and so must the court or tax appeal board) to the *whole* answer to it! Now you proceed to spell out each step in the Value Formula as you did it on this property, and come out at the end with the exact answer. True, you will usually find that most of those in the courtroom haven't the faintest idea what you've been talking about, but you have driven home your point.

Your fee for making an appraisal will vary with the custom in your area, but in general your charge, without going to court or any other type of hearing, will be $200 to $10,000, *plus* $100 to $200 per day for going to court. Going to court includes any days that you are asked to appear, whether the case is called or not, and any day on which you go to court, even if you do not testify because the case is settled in the lobby. Even if you spend 10 minutes in court, you are entitled to be paid for the day. And all you need to know is what you will learn in this book.

The fourth, and by far the most important use of the Value Formula, will be in setting prices and values for your own use in selecting the properties you will buy or reject. In those cases where the buyer asks too much, but wants a counter-offer, you will know exactly how much to offer. Where he has asked a price within the Formula figure, you use your judgment as to whether to offer a little less so as to avoid appearing over-anxious, but you have determined that if the financing can be arranged—you will buy this one. To understand this fourth use we should know a little of the history and customs of Real Estate values.

THE FIFTEEN PER CENT RULE

For hundreds of years there has obtained a custom in our business as to what an investor is entitled to make on his investment. Let us take a simple example.

Suppose X Chain Stores wants to have a store in a certain location. The owner of the land is approached with a proposition. Will he erect a store, 100 feet by 200 feet, and pave a parking lot for 200 cars? If so, how much rent will X Chain have to pay for it?

In figuring out the return on his investment, Mr. Owner must take into account the fact that the building will depreciate as the years pass. That is some loss. Then the money that is invested here cannot be invested elsewhere, and the interest on it is another loss or cost. If the return on his money in the real estate investment is to be only the same or a little more than he would receive as dividends on blue-chip stocks, he is better off buying stocks.

For these reasons the *fifteen per cent rule* gradually became almost universally standard. Here is how it works.

The owner gets quotations from the builder as to the cost of the proposed building. To this he adds the cost of the land. Any other cost, such as the architect's fee, insurance, etc. is added in for a total cost to the owner of the finished store, ready for occupancy. Now the rent per year is fixed by finding a figure that is exactly 15% of the total cost. In this plan, the owner usually pays real estate taxes and has a provision in the lease that any increase will be paid by the tenant, thus leaving the owner, in effect, a guaranteed income. From this, we evolve the general principle:

A piece of Real Estate should earn as annual gross rent, *fifteen per cent* of its cost or value.

Now the Value Formula takes that rule as sound and proven by years of application and experience. It has been the basis for thousands of leases and rentals for generations. The changing value of the dollar has never affected it, of course, because it was a proportionate rule. Thus having established the proportion between the value and the rent, we put the rule to a new use.

Whereas we used to determine the rent to be charged by taking fifteen per cent of the value, we now reverse the process. For it is obvious that if one is true, so is the other. If we accept the principle that a building that cost $100,000 is worth a rental of $15,000 per year, then it is not fair to say that if a building fetches a rental of $15,000 per year, it is worth $100,000? Of course!

But it's not as simple as that. If that were all there were to it, we would not have the advantage that we do over the run-of-the-mill investor. In general, the real estate investor stops right there. That's all he knows about figuring the value and he goes by this rule-of-thumb. It was the way *he* was taught, and he knows no other. What's more, it seems to him quite adequate. As he sees it, this method has proved itself thoroughly. He has been buying property for 19 years with that rule and guide and he has almost always turned a nice profit. What he does NOT realize is that he has been making a nice profit on this or that property these past 19 years, but *not* for the reason that the rule-of-thumb is sound. His profits were made because of the constant rise in prices in the past 19 years! He just about couldn't lose!

You, who will understand the Value Formula will have an enormous advantage over the rule-of-thumb investor. And you will be safe from losses due to inflation or depression. *Your* guide will have its method founded in facts. That is, ALL the facts, not just the gross rent. To understand this, let us consider an example.

Suppose you set out to buy a grocery store. You found two available. One was the Brown Store in Brownsville. The other was the Black Store in Blackstone. You learned the gross income of each. Brown Store took in $5,000 per week. Black Store, likewise, took in $5,000 per week. If you were a rule-of-thumb investor, you would stop right there. That would be all you would need to know. If grocery stores were generally worth six times their gross sales amount, you would place the value of Brown Store at $30,000. You would then compute the value of Black Store the same way and come up with a value of $30,000, too. And, in the natural course of your method, you would fix upon this as the value, so that if the owner of Black Store wanted $35,000, you would refuse to buy it. But if Brown offered you *his* store for $25,000, you would grab it as a bargain—*yes, you would not!*

The most rudimentary understanding of business would make you examine the *facts* about each store much more deeply than that. You would want to know *what part* of the $5,000 that came in each week was profit. What part was used to replace the merchandise sold? How much of the profit went for rent? For help? For other expenses? In other words, you would consider it childishly foolish to place the same value on both stores, simply because the gross sales amount or income was the same. Well, believe it or not, that is nevertheless exactly what thousands of real estate investors do! And that is how millions of dollars worth of real estate is bought and sold every day—by experienced members of this field. That's what they've been doing for years and that's what they will most likely continue to do for generations to come. And that's where you come into the picture with an enormous advantage over them.

When *you* compute the value of a building you start with the amount of gross income—but you only *start there*. Then you take into account all the other factors that will affect your profit and loss picture. For instance, the interest rate on mortgage that you will have to bear will affect your profit and loss figure for decades. We accept as a norm, for purposes of our formula, a rate of 8%, which is the general rate throughout the country in 1973.

But there are many areas where 8 and even 10% mortgages are common. That does not mean these properties are not good buys. But it does mean that the profit you will net will be lower. And that, in turn, means that the price you can afford to pay for the property must be lower if you are to clear a good profit.

Hence the Value Formula takes into account any amount you must pay out each year *over* 8% in mortgage interest as an *excess* expense—over and above the amount we *"forgive"* as normal. If your interest bill is 10% of $50,000 or $4,000 per year instead of $3,000, as it would be at 8%, you will be paying $1,000 more per year in interest than we forgive.

The formula, in these cases, *deducts* that $1,000 from the gross income, and says, in effect, "You are *not* receiving a true gross income of (let us say) $10,000. You are, for *our* purposes, receiving a *true* gross income, before *regular* and *normal* expenses, of $9,000!"

You now do the same process with other facts about this property. You may find that the janitor cost factor is higher than the Formula forgives. If so, you adjust the income for that overcharge. And so on. That is, in effect, the same method that any person with common sense would use in deciding which

grocery store is the best buy. He would study the expense figures, compare them with the income and these would often
lead him to a conclusion he would never have reached otherwise. He might cheerfully pay $35,000 for the Black Store, even
though the gross income was the same as Brown Store, and
Brown could be bought for $25,000. And he would be doing the
right thing.

Let us apply the facts of the grocery example to a true case
in real estate. There are two apartment buildings not far from
my office. They were built on a piece of land that is one-half in
Brookline and one-half in Boston, Mass. The same builder built
both at the same time. He built them precisely alike. As a result, they both earn the same income, approximately $40,000
per year each. Now the rule-of-thumb investor or speculator
stops right there. He takes that income figure of $40,000 and
multiplies it by six and two thirds. That is the same as multiplying 15% as income to bring it to 100% as value. And the speculator buys *either* building at that price, or for as much less as
he can. You will *not* stop there.

Both buildings being exactly the same, they are assessed for
tax purposes for $120,000 each, by their respective cities. But
the tax rate per $1000 of assessed value in Brookline happens
to be $45. That of Boston well over $175. Please fix these facts
firmly in your mind and remember that the annual tax bill for
the Brookline building is some $5,400. That leaves $34,600 of
the income after taxes. The Boston building must pay $21,000
each year as its tax bill, leaving $19,000 of the income for other
purposes. Now I ask you the big question. Would you pay the
same amount for either building? Of course not! Yet, the specu-
lators do! Because their way of figuring does not take these
things into account. Yours does.

The far reaching effects of this method will vitally affect your
fortunes. Here is how.

Let us say there is a building for sale for $15,000. The quickie
rule-of-thumb method indicates that it is worth $17,000. The
untrained speculator gobbles it up, thinking he has found a
bargain. Now he starts to feel the effect of the extraordinarily

large expenses that this particular building carries. He soon finds that he has made a bad buy. He tries to unload it, but, unless he finds another untutored rule-of-thumb user, he must take a loss. Nobody wants to invest in a building and receive NET on his investment, 5 or 6% per year.

The Value Formula, as you apply it to this building, shows a fair buying price of $12,000. When you found you could not buy it at or near this figure, you passed it up. You knew better. Thus you will find the Formula protects you against bad investments. The speculator buys it because he does not know the proper and thorough way to determine what IS a good or bad investment. All he knows is, "multiply the annual income by six and two-thirds and that's what it's worth." So he gets stuck with some real lemons.

It works the other way, too. Let us say the speculator is offered a six-family double Toby for $44,000. The income is only $6,000. He does some quick figuring. He multiplies $6,000 by six and two-thirds. That makes $40,000. So he offers $36,000 or $42,000. You come along and apply the Value Formula. It shows a value of $52,000! You haggle a little and buy it at $48,000. In these cases, the speculator has missed out on some topnotch investments because he used his rule-of-thumb. The Freeman case bears this out.

A speculator whom we will call Jack, offered me the Freeman group of Aunt Tobys. There were four-family and three-family buildings in the lot, fourteen apartments in all. The income in 1946 was about $5,880, with very low-rent-controlled ceilings. The woman who sold them to Jack had been peddling them about for some time and all who came offered her between $23,000 and $25,000, to permit a resale at six and two-third times the annual income with a good profit. Finally Jack had bought it for about $25,000 and set out to sell it at a profit.

He offered it to me. You may be amused to hear what my wife said about the deal when I told her I was considering buying. "Bob, how can you? After all, Jack is a sharpshooter! Don't tell me you expect to get a good buy from him! It doesn't make sense. He's been dealing in properties for years and you'll never convince me that he'd sell it to you at any price that would make it profitable to you." I grinned and reminded her that her roast was smoking.

I bought the parcel for $30,000 with $3,000 down. There was a first mortgage of $24,000 and Jack took a second for $3,000. Application of the Value Formula showed that this property had exceptionally low expense factors. The tenants supplied their own heat and janitor service. Even the hall lights were on the meters of the tenants. Most had occupied the same flat for 25 years or more (shades of Aunt Toby!). They never expected, nor got, any service or attention other than the repair of a leaky roof, a leaky pipe, or an electric fixture. They did their own decorating. In other words, they let the landlord alone and he let them alone and everyone was happy, for years and years. And, most important of all, although these buildings were in neglected condition, the *location* was tops. Thus any improvement was justified and would pay off handsomely. And I would never lack applications from prospective tenants. To this day, I have never seen the inside of half the apartments nor even met those tenants. Each tenant mailed me his rent punctually.

As a result of the fact that I had to pay out so little of the income there was an average of $3,000 yer year left in my hands for the nine years I held it. That makes $27,000. Then I sold it, using the selling methods you will learn here, for $60,000. I was able to prove to a very canny investor that he could buy it at that price and make money, and he did. If I had wanted to sell it a year after buying it, I am certain I could have got $50,000. But at that time I was concentrating on buying—not selling. In the nine years I owned Freeman, I really had a dream investment. The rents came to my office regularly and dependably. I never went to collect a rent in my life. I might drive by the buildings occasionally, say, once a month or even less often, but I wouldn't even slow down. They required a minimum of attention. It was precisely the type of ownership that I had first learned about at Aunt Toby's. But now I was in the Landlord's position. It was just as pleasant as I had dreamed, and more.

In 1955, I sold Freeman and most of my other holdings in a manner and for reasons we shall discuss later. The buyer of Freeman, a Mr. N., paid me $6000 down and gave me a new first mortgage for $54,000 at 4½ per cent on a 22 year basis. In 1955 4½ per cent was a standard interest rate in this area.

Let us total up the whole deal.

I put in, at the purchase		$3,000.
I took out between 1946 and 1955	$ 27,000.00	
I got as down payment from Mr. N.	6,000.00	
My wife and I received payments per month including interest and principal on $54,000 at 4½% for 22 years ... $322.60, which will give us in the 22 years	85,166.40	
that means we will have taken out of Freeman a total of	$118,166.40	
less what we put in	3,000.00	
thus we will clear in the 31 years	$115,166.40	

The one thing that made this possible was simply this: I knew the Value Formula and Jack did not.

Isn't it obvious that if Jack (and his many counterparts) knew the Value Formula, he would have sold Freeman on the basis that I did? We can certainly see from these facts that there must have been many and many a buy that Jack has refused because he uses the old rule-of-thumb, and the price seemed too high for him. Instead, he stuck to a figure that the rule-of-thumb gave him, and, since all the other prospective buyers of Freeman were guided by the same rule, nobody offered the seller more—and the seller took it. But you can see what an advantage it gave me—and will give you.

So we can say that the fourth and most important use of the Value Formula will be to enable you to see good buys that the average speculator does not see, and you will buy them and make the profit that he will pass up. On the other hand, *he* will grab many a "bargain" that you will pass up. After that, unless he is lucky enough to find another as untutored as he himself is, he must take a loss.

That is the importance of the Value Formula and its four main uses.

14

TYPES TO WHICH THE VALUE FORMULA CAN BE APPLIED

The Value Formula necessarily has certain limitations in its application. It is designed only for use in real estate investments for Income. This limits its use clearly. There are several types of investments which some might classify erroneously as real estate investments for income.

When one buys a motel or rooming house, this is a going hotel-type business, not a pure real estate investment for income. The management, care and attention that the owner or operator must apply to his business is far removed from the simple purchase of a rental property. Although an adaptation of the Value Formula has been devised for establishing the value of motels, it must be used cautiously. There are too many variants in the operation of motels. Some are open only in summer, at resort areas. Others only in winter in ski areas. Others year 'round. But certain tax costs, depreciation, interest on investment and other expenses run constant throughout the year. Then again there are many motels which operate swimming pools, restaurants, and even zoos!

Single separate houses, with extremely rare exceptions, are not rental properties bought and held for income. Hence they are not within the class to which the Formula applies. This type is usually bought by a family for a home, and for a figure that you could never afford to pay for it as a rental.

Duplexes and two-family houses are generally in the same class as singles. Occasionally you *will* find one that passes your tests and that you can buy for the figure recommended by the Formula. When this happens you can proceed as if it were an Aunt Toby. But in my experience, such properties are too much in demand by consumers, that is, people who want to live in one side, have almost complete privacy, and enjoy the assistance that the income from the other apartment affords them. Hence you will almost always be outbid.

Blocks of retail stores *are* properties bought for income, generally. However, as has been explained, there is always the serious and imminent danger of their being vacated by storekeepers who have lost business to the Shopping Centers. If your city is one where this is very unlikely, you may buy these but with that risk.

Properties to which the Value Formula applies:

Aunt Tobys.
Four-family houses and those containing more than four families.
Combinations of stores and apartments or offices.
Office buildings.
Industrial buildings, e.g. those containing manufacturers, distributors, plants, etc.
Commercial properties; retail and wholesale service, sales or storage companies.
Shopping Centers.

To apply the Formula to any property (and we speak only about those listed above) we first learn and list certain figures. They are:

The annual gross income (AGI); this is the total amount of rent that comes in from the property when fully rented.
The annual Real Estate tax amount: In areas where a sewer tax or other such tax is assessed in addition to the regular real estate tax, these should be added to form the total annual tax bill for our purposes. Water tax is not included, except in areas where water charges are substantial.
The Interest rate on the mortgage or mortgages that we will carry. This means that you use the interest rate and figure that you will pay on it if you are taking over the old mortgage.

The yearly fuel bill including the supply of hot water, if included. If you are buying a heated property (one in which the landlord furnishes the heat) you should check this figure by seeing the oil bills and statements and obtaining a letter (sent by mail), from the oil supplier. He will want you to continue with him after you buy it, and will gladly furnish the figure. But you want him to send it thru the mail for obvious protective reasons. Ask him for it. He will know what you want.

The Janitor cost (per year) if any. If he resides in an apartment, figure the income from that apartment as if a regular tenant occupied it, and figure the janitor's pay on the basis of the cash he receives, added to the normal rent for the apartment, plus any utilities that you pay for. The total is the true janitor cost. Of course we try to find buildings where no such service is given the tenants, but our formula applies here and when properly used, leads to fine profits.

The yearly cost to the landlord of utilities; Electricity, gas, exterminator, and any other regular and constant cost paid by the owner.

In addition to the above figures you need to know;

Whether there is parking, outdoor or indoor.

Whether there are fourth floor (or higher) walk-up apartments, offices or lofts. As to those buildings which are built up on a perch, where you must climb 15 or more stairs to reach the first floor level, we classify those as if the first floor were the second, etc. Thus, if there is no elevator, we call the third floor the "fourth floor walk-up" for our purposes.

Whether the building is sidewalled on its exterior with wood or any other material that requires paint and care. Brick, concrete, metal and good stucco do not come within this classification.

If the building is an Aunt Toby, or apartment house, whether the tenants must climb a hill as, for instance, from the bus stop, to reach it. As to cities like San Francisco, where practically all property is up on a hill we do not concern ourselves with this point. A tenant will not leave our building for one that is on the level if there ARE no buildings on the level.

The relative location. This will be the only factor in which you must use some judgment, and it will not be difficult. You are asked to grade the location, using the yardstick of the class of quarters you are offering for rent. This has been previously discussed. Have no fear that you can go far wrong on this. You

simply decide (perhaps with your wife's help, and the knowledge of how long the tenants have occupied) whether this
location is going to suit the people you want as tenants. How
well you believe they will be pleased sets the grade. Decide
whether the location for this class of tenant is:

> Excellent
> Good
> Fair.

The only time we are concerned with grades lower than this
is for appraisal purposes—not for the purpose of buying for
ourselves.

The grades to be used only for appraisal purposes are:

> Poor
> Undesirable; very poor
> Decayed or slum.

Here is the form we use for our Formula:

Section I

Step 1. Find Annual Working Income:
Enter Gross Yearly Rents here . . . . $_____

Yearly Taxes and Utilities supplied
(*For furnished apts. see below)
enter total here . . . . $_____

Deduct Tax & Utility total from
Gross Rents

Balance is *annual working income*
(*AWI*) enter here . . . . $_____

*Step 2. List Above-normal Expenses. Fuel
& Loss Factors.*
Enter any Annual Mortgage Inter-
est above 8% here . . . . $_____

Enter any janitor cost above 7% of
AWI here . . . .   _____

If Wooden Exterior enter 10% of
ANNUAL WORKING INCOME
(AWI) here . . . .   _____

If Building is reached by hillclimb
enter 7% of ANNUAL WORKING
INCOME here . . . .   _____

* Where furnishings are supplied with apartments include annual cost of
replacing and repairing furniture and furnishings.

DEDUCTION FOR LOCATION:
For Excellent Location 0% of AWI
For Good Location... 5% of AWI
For Fair Location....10% of AWI
For Poor Location....25% of AWI
For Very Poor
    Location .... 40% of AWI
For Decayed or Slum
    Location ....50% of AWI $_____

(If Heated) Enter Entire Fuel Bill Here... $_____
If building contains 4th floor
walk-ups enter 20% of the 4th
floor rents here ....   _____
If building contains 5th floor
walk-ups enter 30% of the 5th
floor rents here ....   _____

Step 3.   Add all items in Step 2 and enter total here... $_____

*Step 4.   Subtract from Annual Working Income. Balance   Box PAI
is Primary Adjusted Income. Enter here*...... $_____

Section II   Addition of Extra Profit Items and Factors

Step 5.   List Extra Profit Items and Factors
Any mortgage interest saving under 8% enter
annual saving here .... $_____
If Parking or Garages available, 1 per tenant,
whether free or not. For Parking enter 5%;
for Garages 8% of AWI ....   _____
If Janitor Service is not supplied enter 5%
of AWI here ....   _____
If all electric bills are paid by the tenant
enter 2% of AWI here ....   _____

*Step 6.   Add total of all items in Section II including
PAI. Total is Final Adjusted Income. Enter here*   _____

*Step 7.   Multiply Final Adjusted Income by 6% (or
divide by 3 and multiply by 20). Result is
GROSS VALUE. Enter here* ....   _____

*Step 8.   Enter cost of repairs required to put property
in reasonable condition here* ....   _____

*Step 9.   Deduct cost of repairs from Gross Value.
Balance is Fair Market Value of Property.
Enter here* ....   _____

Copyright 1960. Order these forms direct from: Real forms, Box 1, Brookline, Mass.

Let us *do* the Value Formula for a typical Aunt Toby unheated and for a heated one to see how it works. Here are the figures on the Freeman group of Aunt Tobys as they were presented to me by Jack.

Income rents per year $5,880

Taxes $721
Water   60
Insurance   113

1st Mortgage, Interest, and Principal $24,000 at 4%
(standard rate in those days) 20 year basis $1,752.48

Interest and Principal on 2nd mortgage at 4%, 10 years   364.56

There was no janitor service, heat, nor even decoration supplied by the owner.

The location was excellent by the yardstick of *this* price and standard of apartment. There were no apartments above the third floor (2 flights of stairs) level lot. No hill climb. 3, 4, and 5 room apartments. Plenty of open air parking.

Value Formula for 126 Browne St. and 214 through 222 Freeman St.

Section I

Step 1. Find Annual Working Income (this is called AWI)

     Gross yearly rental income $5,880.00
     Deduct: taxes and utilities supplied   721.00

Annual Working Income .... $ 5,159.00

Step 2. List Above-Normal Expenses and Loss Factors:

     Yearly Mortgage Interest above 6% (my mortgages were 4% at that time) .... $ 00.00

     If wood exterior (they were) 10% of AWI 515.90

     If Building contains 4th floor walk-ups (there were none) 00.00

If building is reached by a hillclimb
place 7% of Annual Working
Income here 00.00
Deduct for Location: Excellent
Location—0% 00.00

Step 3. ADD items in Step 2 and place total here .. $ 515.90

Step 4. Deduct total from Annual Working Income.
This is the Primary Adjusted Income, place in   PAI
PAI here 4,643.10

Section II. Addition of Extra-Profit Factors

Step 5. List extra-profit factors
Any Mortgage Interest saving *under* 6%* (2%
of 27,000 per year) 540.00
If parking or garages available (There is parking) (5% of AWI) 257.95
If all electric bills are paid by tenants (they
are) 2% of AWI 103.18

Step 6. Add PAI and items in Step 5, place total here.
This is *final adjusted income* .... $ 5,544.23

Step 7. Multiply *final adjusted income* by 6% (or divide by 3 and multiply by 20). Result is
Gross Value $36,961.40

Step 8. Place cost of repairs required to put property
in reasonable condition here 600.00

Step 9. Deduct cost of repairs from *gross value.* Balance is *fair market value of property* $36,361.40

Having established that I could safely pay $37,000 for this
property and make a fine return on my investment, I "figured
the net" on the property to learn just how much I would clear
net in hand if I offered and paid $30,000. We will soon do just
that on this unheated Aunt Toby, but at the moment we are
concerned with the application of the Value Formula to a
heated property. Let us apply the Value Formula to No. 16
which I bought from Mr. L.

The facts and figures on No. 16 (at that time) were:

Eleven four room suites renting for $39 to $49. (These rents were
then controlled at this level.) Owner supplied heat, but not
hot water nor janitor service.

Small level lot with parking. Three suites were fourth floor
walkups.

There was a part-time janitor who took care of snow, put out
the rubbish barrels for collection and no more. He was paid
$15 per month.

Value Formula for 16 High St., Brookline. Heated Property.

Section I

Step 1. Find Annual Working Income;

Enter Gross yearly rents here . .	$6,000.00	
Deduct-Yearly taxes	807	
Electric for halls	71	
Total	$ 878.00	
Balance is *Annual working income* (AWI) ..		$ 5,122.00

Step 2. List above-normal Expenses, Fuel
and Loss Factors;

Enter any mortgage interest above 6%*	$ 00.00
Enter any janitor cost above 7% AWI	00.00
If wooden exterior 10% of AWI ...	00.00
If Building is reached by hillclimb 7% of AWI	00.00
Deduction for Location: Rated Excellent	00.00
Entire annual fuel bill	715.00
If Building contains 4th floor walkups enter 20% of 4th floor rents here	252.00

Step 3. Add All Items in Step 2 and enter total here ..   967.00

Step 4. Subtract Above Normal expenses, etc. from
Annual Working Income. This is *primary adjusted income*. Enter in Box PAI here ......   **PAI** $ 4,155.00

Section II. Addition of Extra Profit Items and Factors

Step 5. List extra profit items and factors;
Any mortgage interest saving *under* 6%* 1½%
of $19,000 ....   285.00
If Parking available 5% of AWI 256.10
If Janitor Service NOT supplied 5% of AWI
(we do supply partial service)
If all electric bills are paid by tenants (they
aren't).

Step 6. Add all items in Sec. 2 including PAI. Total is
final adjusted income. Enter here .... $ 4,696.10

Step 7. Multiply Final Adjusted Income by 6% (or divide by 3 and multiply by 20). Result is *gross
value.* Enter here .... ⁄ $31,307.32

Step 8. Enter cost of repairs required to put property
in reasonable condition here 00.00

Step 9. Deduct cost of repairs needed from Gross
Value. Balance is *fair market value of property* $31,307.32

Now it becomes apparent why Mr. L would not have been permitted to walk out of my office without having signed up even had he insisted on 26, 28, or $30,000. When we do the Net in Hand calculation, it will be even more apparent.

It should be borne in mind that the interest rates noted above were current and normal in this area at the time I bought these properties. Of course, they are not now available, nor are taxes as low as they were then. Fuel costs much more today too. But by the same token, rents are substantially higher too and it all balances out beautifully.

15

FIGURING THE NET

Having established through the Value Formula *what we can pay* for a building, we must determine whether this building will "carry itself" at this price. This process now becomes relatively simple, but is necessary before we can present a definite offer to the seller. Our Value Formula has produced a figure that is recommended but we cannot proceed until we have tested the figure for gross and net income. To be attractive, a property should show good prospects of paying all its carrying expense, all mortgage interest AND principal payments, and leave us *net clear in hand,* 25 to 33 per cent of the amount we originally invested (including any amounts we had to pay to put the property in fair condition).

This net in hand is called in the vernacular, MIF or "money in fist." From this MIF amount, we must occasionally stand a loss through vacancy, which we will soon learn to hold to a tiny minimum, and we must contribute to the repair fund when it is short of the sum needed to make a major repair such as a new roof or heater. However, this happens very seldom.

Here is the form for determining the NET or MIF.

Total yearly rents .... $_____
    Payouts:
        Taxes .... $_____
        Fuel .... _____

Other utilities supplied (such as gas,
    light, etc.) ....   ———
Janitor cost ....   ———
Insurance ....   ———
Water ....   ———
Total annual mortgage payments, in-
    cluding Interest and Principal on all
    mortgages ....   ———

Deduct payouts from total rents. Balance
is Net in Hand (MIF) as would be
carrying them in accordance with our
offer.

Total Payouts $———   .... $———
    Net in Hand .... $———

CALCULATING MORTGAGE PAYMENTS

At this time we should learn how to use a mortgage payment
calculator. Practically every bank in the United States and
Canada uses the flat payment plan. You will meet it in all the
mortgages you undertake.

Whenever you want to buy with a second mortgage you will
refer to your calculator to determine precisely the flat amount
you pay each month, which will include interest and principal
payment and will automatically pay off the obligation in the
prescribed number of years.

Similarly, when you contemplate making an offer for a
building, you will be setting forth that you will buy it, *providing* you can obtain:

> a certain amount of mortgage
> at a certain per cent of interest
> for a certain number of years.

These are the three terms of any loan that you need to know in
order to determine quickly the payments per month.

If, for instance, you plan to offer $20,000 for the building
with $3,000 down, providing you can obtain a mortgage loan of
$17,000 at 8% for 20 years, you will want to know how much
you will be paying out each month to detemine the MIF. You

can look it up in seconds. The payment is $142.19 per month. Now it is multiplied by 12 to determine the gross amount per year you will be paying out to the bank for interest and principal.

The calculator booklets are for sale at most law stationers and some banks give them to customers free.* If there is no near supplier, the mortgage officer of the bank will refer you to one.

Here is a chart covering most of the amounts and percentages that you will require. If the loan is an uneven amount like 12,300, you first find the payment for $12,000 and add the payment for $300 and the total will be the monthly payment for $12,300.

MONTHLY PAYMENT

6% NECESSARY TO AMORTIZE A LOAN 6%

Term Amount	10 Years	11 Years	12 Years	13 Years	14 Years	15 Years	16 Years	17 Years
$5600	62.18	58.06	54.65	51.79	49.35	47.26	45.45	43.86
5700	63.29	59.10	55.63	52.71	50.24	48.10	46.26	44.64
5800	64.40	60.13	56.60	53.64	51.12	48.95	47.07	45.42
5900	65.51	61.17	57.58	54.56	52.00	49.79	47.88	46.21
6000	66.62	62.21	58.56	55.49	52.88	50.64	48.69	46.99
6100	67.73	63.24	59.53	56.41	53.76	51.48	49.50	47.77
6200	68.84	64.28	60.51	57.34	54.64	52.32	50.31	48.56
6300	69.95	65.32	61.48	58.26	55.52	53.17	51.13	49.34
6400	71.06	66.35	62.46	59.19	56.40	54.01	51.94	50.12
6500	72.17	67.39	63.44	60.11	57.29	54.86	52.75	50.91
6600	73.28	68.43	64.41	61.04	58.17	55.70	53.56	51.69
6700	74.39	69.46	65.39	61.98	59.05	56.54	54.37	52.47
6800	75.50	70.50	66.36	62.89	59.93	57.39	55.18	53.26
6900	76.61	71.54	67.34	63.81	60.81	58.23	55.99	54.04
7000	77.72	72.57	68.31	64.74	61.69	59.07	56.81	54.82
7100	78.83	73.61	69.29	65.66	62.57	59.92	57.62	55.61
7200	79.94	74.65	70.27	66.59	63.45	60.76	58.43	56.39
7300	81.05	75.68	71.24	67.51	64.34	61.61	59.24	57.17
7400	82.16	76.72	72.22	68.43	65.22	62.45	60.05	57.95
7500	83.27	77.76	73.19	69.36	66.10	63.29	60.86	58.74
7600	84.38	78.79	74.17	70.28	66.98	64.14	61.67	59.52
7700	85.49	79.83	75.15	71.21	67.86	64.98	62.49	60.30
7800	86.60	80.87	76.12	72.13	68.74	65.83	63.30	61.09
7900	87.71	81.90	77.10	73.06	69.62	66.67	64.11	61.87
8000	88.82	82.94	78.07	73.98	70.50	67.51	64.92	62.65

(*continued on following page*)

* Or send $2.00 for complete booklet to: Realforms, P.O. Box 1, Brookline, Mass. 02146.

MONTHLY PAYMENT
NECESSARY TO AMORTIZE A LOAN **7.00%**

$ AMT	18 YRS	20 YRS	22 YRS	25 YRS	30 YRS	35 YRS	40 YRS
100	0.82	0.78	0.74	0.71	0.67	0.64	0.62
200	1.63	1.55	1.49	1.41	1.33	1.28	1.24
300	2.45	2.33	2.23	2.12	2.00	1.92	1.86
400	3.26	3.10	2.97	2.83	2.66	2.56	2.49
500	4.08	3.88	3.72	3.53	3.33	3.19	3.11
600	4.89	4.65	4.46	4.24	3.99	3.83	3.73
700	5.71	5.43	5.20	4.95	4.66	4.47	4.35
800	6.52	6.20	5.95	5.65	5.32	5.11	4.97
900	7.34	6.98	6.69	6.36	5.99	5.75	5.59
1000	8.16	7.75	7.43	7.07	6.65	6.39	6.21
1500	12.23	11.63	11.15	10.60	9.98	9.58	9.32
2000	16.31	15.51	14.87	14.14	13.31	12.78	12.43
2500	20.39	19.38	18.59	17.67	16.63	15.97	15.54
3000	24.47	23.26	22.30	21.20	19.96	19.17	18.64
3500	28.54	27.14	26.02	24.74	23.29	22.36	21.75
4000	32.62	31.01	29.74	28.27	26.61	25.55	24.86
4500	36.70	34.89	33.45	31.81	29.94	28.75	27.96
5000	40.78	38.76	37.17	35.34	33.27	31.94	31.07
5500	44.85	42.64	40.89	38.87	36.59	35.14	34.18
6000	48.93	46.52	44.61	42.41	39.92	38.33	37.29
6500	53.01	50.39	48.32	45.94	43.24	41.53	40.39
7000	57.09	54.27	52.04	49.47	46.57	44.72	43.50
7500	61.16	58.15	55.76	53.01	49.90	47.91	46.61
8000	65.24	62.02	59.47	56.54	53.22	51.11	49.71
8500	69.32	65.90	63.19	60.08	56.55	54.30	52.82
9000	73.40	69.78	66.91	63.61	59.88	57.50	55.93
9500	77.47	73.65	70.63	67.14	63.20	60.69	59.04
10000	81.55	77.53	74.34	70.68	66.53	63.89	62.14
10500	85.63	81.41	78.06	74.21	69.86	67.08	65.25
11000	89.71	85.28	81.78	77.75	73.18	70.27	68.36
11500	93.78	89.16	85.49	81.28	76.51	73.47	71.46
12000	97.86	93.04	89.21	84.81	79.84	76.66	74.57
12500	101.94	96.91	92.93	88.35	83.16	79.86	77.68
13000	106.02	100.79	96.65	91.88	86.49	83.05	80.79
13500	110.09	104.67	100.36	95.42	89.82	86.25	83.89
14000	114.17	108.54	104.08	98.95	93.14	89.44	87.00
14500	118.25	112.42	107.80	102.48	96.47	92.63	90.11
15000	122.33	116.29	111.51	106.02	99.80	95.83	93.21
15500	126.40	120.17	115.23	109.55	103.12	99.02	96.32
16000	130.48	124.05	118.95	113.08	106.45	102.22	99.43
16500	134.56	127.92	122.66	116.62	109.77	105.41	102.54
17000	138.64	131.80	126.38	120.15	113.10	108.61	105.64
17500	142.71	135.68	130.10	123.69	116.43	111.80	108.75
18000	146.79	139.55	133.82	127.22	119.75	114.99	111.86
18500	150.87	143.43	137.53	130.75	123.08	118.19	114.96
19000	154.95	147.31	141.25	134.29	126.41	121.38	118.07
19500	159.02	151.18	144.97	137.82	129.73	124.58	121.18
20000	163.10	155.06	148.68	141.36	133.06	127.77	124.29
20500	167.18	158.94	152.40	144.89	136.39	130.97	127.39
21000	171.26	162.81	156.12	148.42	139.71	134.16	130.50
21500	175.33	166.69	159.84	151.96	143.04	137.35	133.61
22000	179.41	170.57	163.55	155.49	146.37	140.55	136.71
22500	183.49	174.44	167.27	159.03	149.69	143.74	139.82
23000	187.57	178.32	170.99	162.56	153.02	146.94	142.93
23500	191.64	182.20	174.70	166.09	156.35	150.13	146.04
24000	195.72	186.07	178.42	169.63	159.67	153.33	149.14
24500	199.80	189.95	182.14	173.16	163.00	156.52	152.25
25000	203.88	193.82	185.86	176.69	166.33	159.71	155.36
26000	212.03	201.58	193.29	183.76	172.98	166.10	161.57
27000	220.19	209.33	200.72	190.83	179.63	172.49	167.79
28000	228.34	217.08	208.16	197.90	186.28	178.88	174.00
29000	236.50	224.84	215.59	204.97	192.94	185.27	180.22
30000	244.65	232.59	223.03	212.03	199.59	191.66	186.43
35000	285.43	271.35	260.20	247.37	232.86	223.60	217.50
40000	326.20	310.12	297.37	282.71	266.12	255.54	248.57

MONTHLY PAYMENT
NECESSARY TO AMORTIZE A LOAN　　7.25%

$ AMT	18 YRS	20 YRS	22 YRS	25 YRS	30 YRS	35 YRS	40 YRS
100	0.83	0.79	0.76	0.72	0.68	0.66	0.64
200	1.66	1.58	1.52	1.45	1.36	1.31	1.28
300	2.49	2.37	2.28	2.17	2.05	1.97	1.92
400	3.32	3.16	3.04	2.89	2.73	2.63	2.56
500	4.15	3.95	3.79	3.61	3.41	3.28	3.20
600	4.98	4.74	4.55	4.34	4.09	3.94	3.84
700	5.81	5.53	5.31	5.06	4.78	4.60	4.48
800	6.64	6.32	6.07	5.78	5.46	5.25	5.12
900	7.47	7.11	6.83	6.51	6.14	5.91	5.76
1000	8.30	7.90	7.59	7.23	6.82	6.56	6.40
1500	12.45	11.86	11.38	10.84	10.23	9.85	9.60
2000	16.60	15.81	15.18	14.46	13.64	13.13	12.79
2500	20.75	19.76	18.97	18.07	17.05	16.41	15.99
3000	24.91	23.71	22.77	21.68	20.47	19.69	19.19
3500	29.06	27.66	26.56	25.30	23.88	22.98	22.39
4000	33.21	31.62	30.36	28.91	27.29	26.26	25.59
4500	37.36	35.57	34.15	32.53	30.70	29.54	28.79
5000	41.51	39.52	37.94	36.14	34.11	32.82	31.98
5500	45.66	43.47	41.74	39.75	37.52	36.11	35.18
6000	49.81	47.42	45.53	43.37	40.93	39.39	38.38
6500	53.96	51.37	49.33	46.98	44.34	42.67	41.58
7000	58.11	55.33	53.12	50.60	47.75	45.95	44.78
7500	62.26	59.28	56.92	54.21	51.16	49.24	47.98
8000	66.41	63.23	60.71	57.82	54.57	52.52	51.17
8500	70.56	67.18	64.51	61.44	57.98	55.80	54.37
9000	74.72	71.13	68.30	65.05	61.40	59.08	57.57
9500	78.87	75.09	72.09	68.67	64.81	62.36	60.77
10000	83.02	79.04	75.89	72.28	68.22	65.65	63.97
10500	87.17	82.99	79.68	75.89	71.63	68.93	67.17
11000	91.32	86.94	83.48	79.51	75.04	72.21	70.36
11500	95.47	90.89	87.27	83.12	78.45	75.49	73.56
12000	99.62	94.85	91.07	86.74	81.86	78.78	76.76
12500	103.77	98.80	94.86	90.35	85.27	82.06	79.96
13000	107.92	102.75	98.66	93.96	88.68	85.34	83.16
13500	112.07	106.70	102.45	97.58	92.09	88.62	86.36
14000	116.22	110.65	106.25	101.19	95.50	91.91	89.55
14500	120.37	114.60	110.04	104.81	98.92	95.19	92.75
15000	124.53	118.56	113.83	108.42	102.33	98.47	95.95
15500	128.68	122.51	117.63	112.04	105.74	101.75	99.15
16000	132.83	126.46	121.42	115.65	109.15	105.03	102.35
16500	136.98	130.41	125.22	119.26	112.56	108.32	105.55
17000	141.13	134.36	129.01	122.88	115.97	111.60	108.74
17500	145.28	138.32	132.81	126.49	119.38	114.88	111.94
18000	149.43	142.27	136.60	130.11	122.79	118.16	115.14
18500	153.58	146.22	140.40	133.72	126.20	121.45	118.34
19000	157.73	150.17	144.19	137.33	129.61	124.73	121.54
19500	161.88	154.12	147.98	140.95	133.02	128.01	124.74
10000	166.03	158.08	151.78	144.56	136.44	131.29	127.93
20500	170.19	162.03	155.57	148.18	139.85	134.58	131.13
21000	174.34	165.98	159.37	151.79	143.26	137.86	134.33
21500	178.49	169.93	163.16	155.40	146.67	141.14	137.53
22000	182.64	173.88	166.96	159.02	150.08	144.42	140.73
22500	186.79	177.83	170.75	162.63	153.49	147.71	143.93
23000	190.94	181.79	174.55	166.25	156.90	150.99	147.12
23500	195.09	185.74	178.34	169.86	160.31	154.27	150.32
24000	199.24	189.69	182.13	173.47	163.72	157.55	153.52
24500	203.39	193.64	185.93	177.09	167.13	160.83	156.72
25000	207.54	197.59	189.72	180.70	170.54	164.12	159.92
26000	215.84	205.50	197.31	187.93	177.37	170.68	166.31
27000	224.15	213.40	204.90	195.16	184.19	177.25	172.71
28000	232.45	221.31	212.49	202.39	191.01	183.81	179.11
29000	240.75	229.21	220.08	209.61	197.83	190.38	185.50
30000	249.05	237.11	227.67	216.84	204.65	196.94	191.90
35000	290.56	276.63	265.61	252.98	238.76	229.76	223.89
40000	332.07	316.15	303.56	289.12	272.87	262.59	255.87

MONTHLY PAYMENT
NECESSARY TO AMORTIZE A LOAN 7.50%

$ AMT	18 YRS	20 YRS	22 YRS	25 YRS	30 YRS	35 YRS	40 YRS
100	0.84	0.81	0.77	0.74	0.70	0.67	0.66
200	1.69	1.61	1.55	1.48	1.40	1.35	1.32
300	2.53	2.42	2.32	2.22	2.10	2.02	1.97
400	3.38	3.22	3.10	2.96	2.80	2.70	2.63
500	4.22	4.03	3.87	3.69	3.50	3.37	3.29
600	5.07	4.83	4.65	4.43	4.20	4.05	3.95
700	5.91	5.64	5.42	5.17	4.89	4.72	4.61
800	6.76	6.44	6.20	5.91	5.59	5.39	5.26
900	7.60	7.25	6.97	6.65	6.29	6.07	5.92
1000	8.45	8.06	7.75	7.39	6.99	6.74	6.58
1500	12.67	12.08	11.62	11.08	10.49	10.11	9.87
2000	16.90	16.11	15.49	14.78	13.98	13.48	13.16
2500	21.12	20.14	19.36	18.47	17.48	16.86	16.45
3000	25.35	24.17	23.24	22.17	20.98	20.23	19.74
3500	29.57	28.20	27.11	25.86	24.47	23.60	23.03
4000	33.80	32.22	30.98	29.56	27.97	26.97	26.32
4500	38.02	36.25	34.85	33.25	31.46	30.34	29.61
5000	42.25	40.28	38.73	36.95	34.96	33.71	32.90
5500	46.47	44.31	42.60	40.64	38.46	37.08	36.19
6000	50.70	48.34	46.47	44.34	41.95	40.45	39.48
6500	54.92	52.36	50.34	48.03	45.45	43.83	42.77
7000	59.15	56.39	54.22	51.73	48.95	47.20	46.06
7500	63.37	60.42	58.09	55.42	52.44	50.57	49.36
8000	67.60	64.45	61.96	59.12	55.94	53.94	52.65
8500	71.82	68.48	65.83	62.81	59.43	57.31	55.94
9000	76.05	72.50	69.71	66.51	62.93	60.68	59.23
9500	80.27	76.53	73.58	70.20	66.43	64.05	62.52
10000	84.50	80.56	77.45	73.90	69.92	67.42	65.81
10500	88.72	84.59	81.32	77.59	73.42	70.80	69.10
11000	92.95	88.62	85.20	81.29	76.91	74.17	72.39
11500	97.17	92.64	89.07	84.98	80.41	77.54	75.68
12000	101.40	96.67	92.94	88.68	83.91	80.91	78.97
12500	105.62	100.70	96.81	92.37	87.40	84.28	82.26
13000	109.85	104.73	100.69	96.07	90.90	87.65	85.55
13500	114.07	108.76	104.56	99.76	94.39	91.02	88.84
14000	118.30	112.78	108.43	103.46	97.89	94.39	92.13
14500	122.52	116.81	112.30	107.15	101.39	97.77	95.42
15000	126.75	120.84	116.18	110.85	104.88	101.14	98.71
15500	130.97	124.87	120.05	114.54	108.38	104.51	102.00
16000	135.20	128.89	123.92	118.24	111.87	107.88	105.29
16500	139.42	132.92	127.79	121.93	115.37	111.25	108.58
17000	143.65	136.95	131.67	125.63	118.87	114.62	111.87
17500	147.87	140.98	135.54	129.32	122.36	117.99	115.16
18000	152.10	145.01	139.41	133.02	125.86	121.36	118.45
18500	156.32	149.03	143.28	136.71	129.35	124.73	121.74
19000	160.54	153.06	147.16	140.41	132.85	128.11	125.03
19500	164.77	157.09	151.03	144.10	136.35	131.48	128.32
20000	168.99	161.12	154.90	147.80	139.84	134.85	131.61
20500	173.22	165.15	158.77	151.49	143.34	138.22	134.90
21000	177.44	169.17	162.65	155.19	146.84	141.59	138.19
21500	181.67	173.20	166.52	158.88	150.33	144.96	141.49
22000	185.89	177.23	170.39	162.58	153.83	148.33	144.78
22500	190.12	181.26	174.26	166.27	157.32	151.70	148.07
23000	194.34	185.29	178.14	169.97	160.82	155.08	151.36
23500	198.57	189.31	182.01	173.66	164.32	158.45	154.65
24000	202.79	193.34	185.88	177.36	167.81	161.82	157.94
24500	207.02	197.37	189.76	181.05	171.31	165.19	161.23
25000	211.24	201.40	193.63	184.75	174.80	168.56	164.52
26000	219.69	209.45	201.37	192.14	181.80	175.30	171.10
27000	228.14	217.51	209.12	199.53	188.79	182.05	177.68
28000	236.59	225.57	216.86	206.92	195.78	188.79	184.26
29000	245.04	233.62	224.61	214.31	202.77	195.53	190.84
30000	253.49	241.68	232.35	221.70	209.76	202.27	197.42
35000	295.74	281.96	271.08	258.65	244.73	235.98	230.32
40000	337.99	322.24	309.80	295.60	279.69	269.70	263.23

MONTHLY PAYMENT
NECESSARY TO AMORTIZE A LOAN 7.75%

$ AMT	18 YRS	20 YRS	22 YRS	25 YRS	30 YRS	35 YRS	40 YRS
100	0.86	0.82	0.79	0.76	0.72	0.69	0.68
200	1.72	1.64	1.58	1.51	1.43	1.38	1.35
300	2.58	2.46	2.37	2.27	2.15	2.08	2.03
400	3.44	3.28	3.16	3.02	2.87	2.77	2.71
500	4.30	4.10	3.95	3.78	3.58	3.46	3.38
600	5.16	4.93	4.74	4.53	4.30	4.15	4.06
700	6.02	5.75	5.53	5.29	5.01	4.85	4.74
800	6.88	6.57	6.32	6.04	5.73	5.54	5.41
900	7.74	7.39	7.11	6.80	6.45	6.23	6.09
1000	8.60	8.21	7.90	7.55	7.16	6.92	6.77
1500	12.90	12.31	11.85	11.33	10.75	10.38	10.15
2000	17.20	16.42	15.81	15.11	14.33	13.84	13.53
2500	21.50	20.52	19.76	18.88	17.91	17.30	16.92
3000	25.80	24.63	23.71	22.66	21.49	20.77	20.30
3500	30.10	28.73	27.66	26.44	25.07	24.23	23.68
4000	34.40	32.84	31.61	30.21	28.66	27.69	27.06
4500	38.70	36.94	35.56	33.99	32.24	31.15	30.45
5000	43.00	41.05	39.51	37.77	35.82	34.61	33.83
5500	47.29	45.15	43.47	41.54	39.40	38.07	37.21
6000	51.59	49.26	47.42	45.32	42.98	41.53	40.60
6500	55.89	53.36	51.37	49.10	46.57	44.99	43.98
7000	60.19	57.47	55.32	52.87	50.15	48.45	47.36
7500	64.49	61.57	59.27	56.65	53.73	51.91	50.75
8000	68.79	65.68	63.22	60.43	57.31	55.37	54.13
8500	73.09	69.78	67.17	64.20	60.90	58.83	57.51
9000	77.39	73.89	71.12	67.98	64.48	62.30	60.90
9500	81.69	77.99	75.08	71.76	68.06	65.76	64.28
10000	85.99	82.09	79.03	75.53	71.64	69.22	67.66
10500	90.29	86.20	82.98	79.31	75.22	72.68	71.05
11000	94.59	90.30	86.93	83.09	78.81	76.14	74.43
11500	98.89	94.41	90.88	86.86	82.39	79.60	77.81
12000	103.19	98.51	94.83	90.64	85.97	83.06	81.19
12500	107.49	102.62	98.78	94.42	89.55	86.52	84.58
13000	111.79	106.72	102.74	98.19	93.13	89.98	87.96
13500	116.09	110.83	106.69	101.97	96.72	93.44	91.34
14000	120.39	114.93	110.64	105.75	100.30	96.90	94.73
14500	124.69	119.04	114.59	109.52	103.88	100.37	98.11
15000	128.99	123.14	118.54	113.30	107.46	103.83	101.49
15500	133.29	127.25	122.49	117.08	111.04	107.29	104.88
16000	137.58	131.35	126.44	120.85	114.63	110.75	108.26
16500	141.88	135.46	130.40	124.63	118.21	114.21	111.64
17000	146.18	139.56	134.35	128.41	121.79	117.67	115.03
17500	150.48	143.67	138.30	132.18	125.37	121.13	118.41
18000	154.78	147.77	142.25	135.96	128.95	124.59	121.79
18500	159.08	151.88	146.20	139.74	132.54	128.05	125.17
19000	163.38	155.98	150.15	143.51	136.12	131.51	128.56
19500	167.68	160.08	154.10	147.29	139.70	134.97	131.94
20000	171.98	164.19	158.05	151.07	143.28	138.44	135.32
20500	176.28	168.29	162.01	154.84	146.86	141.90	138.71
21000	180.58	172.40	165.96	158.62	150.45	145.36	142.09
21500	184.88	176.50	169.91	162.40	154.03	148.82	145.47
22000	189.18	180.61	173.86	166.17	157.61	152.28	148.86
22500	193.48	184.71	177.81	169.95	161.19	155.74	152.24
23000	197.78	188.82	181.76	173.73	164.77	159.20	155.62
23500	202.08	192.92	185.71	177.50	168.36	162.66	159.01
24000	206.38	197.03	189.67	181.28	171.94	166.12	162.39
24500	210.68	201.13	193.62	185.06	175.52	169.58	165.77
25000	214.98	205.24	197.57	188.83	179.10	173.04	169.15
26000	223.58	213.45	205.47	196.39	186.27	179.97	175.92
27000	232.17	221.66	213.37	203.94	193.43	186.89	182.69
28000	240.77	229.87	221.28	211.49	200.60	193.81	189.45
29000	249.37	238.08	229.18	219.05	207.76	200.73	196.22
30000	257.97	246.28	237.08	226.60	214.92	207.65	202.99
35000	300.97	287.33	276.60	264.37	250.74	242.26	236.82
40000	343.96	328.38	316.11	302.13	286.56	276.87	270.65

MONTHLY PAYMENT
NECESSARY TO AMORTIZE A LOAN   8.00%

$ AMT	18 YRS	20 YRS	22 YRS	25 YRS	30 YRS	35 YRS	40 YRS
100	0.87	0.84	0.81	0.77	0.73	0.71	0.70
200	1.75	1.67	1.61	1.54	1.47	1.42	1.39
300	2.62	2.51	2.42	2.32	2.20	2.13	2.09
400	3.50	3.35	3.22	3.09	2.94	2.84	2.78
500	4.37	4.18	4.03	3.86	3.67	3.55	3.48
600	5.25	5.02	4.84	4.63	4.40	4.26	4.17
700	6.12	5.86	5.64	5.40	5.14	4.97	4.87
800	7.00	6.69	6.45	6.17	5.87	5.68	5.56
900	7.87	7.53	7.26	6.95	6.60	6.39	6.26
1000	8.75	8.36	8.06	7.72	7.34	7.10	6.95
1500	13.12	12.55	12.09	11.58	11.01	10.65	10.43
2000	17.50	16.73	16.12	15.44	14.68	14.21	13.91
2500	21.87	20.91	20.15	19.30	18.34	17.76	17.38
3000	26.25	25.09	24.19	23.15	22.01	21.31	20.86
3500	30.62	29.28	28.22	27.01	25.68	24.86	24.34
4000	35.00	33.46	32.25	30.87	29.35	28.41	27.81
4500	39.37	37.64	36.28	34.73	33.02	31.96	31.29
5000	43.75	41.82	40.31	38.59	36.69	35.51	34.77
5500	48.12	46.00	44.34	42.45	40.36	39.06	38.24
6000	52.50	50.19	48.37	46.31	44.03	42.62	41.72
6500	56.87	54.37	52.40	50.17	47.69	46.17	45.20
7000	61.25	58.55	56.43	54.03	51.36	49.72	48.67
7500	65.62	62.73	60.46	57.89	55.03	53.27	52.15
8000	70.00	66.92	64.49	61.75	58.70	56.82	55.62
8500	74.37	71.10	68.53	65.60	62.37	60.37	59.10
9000	78.75	75.28	72.56	69.46	66.04	63.92	62.58
9500	83.12	79.46	76.59	73.32	69.71	67.47	66.05
10000	87.50	83.64	80.62	77.18	73.38	71.03	69.53
10500	91.87	87.83	84.65	81.04	77.05	74.58	73.01
11000	96.25	92.01	88.68	84.90	80.71	78.13	76.48
11500	100.62	96.19	92.71	88.76	84.38	81.68	79.96
12000	105.00	100.37	96.74	92.62	88.05	85.23	83.44
12500	109.37	104.56	100.77	96.48	91.72	88.78	86.91
13000	113.75	108.74	104.80	100.34	95.39	92.33	90.39
13500	118.12	112.92	108.83	104.20	99.06	95.89	93.87
14000	122.49	117.10	112.86	108.05	102.73	99.44	97.34
14500	126.87	121.28	116.90	111.91	106.40	102.99	100.82
15000	131.24	125.47	120.93	115.77	110.06	106.54	104.30
15500	135.62	129.65	124.96	119.63	113.73	110.09	107.77
16000	139.99	133.83	128.99	123.49	117.40	113.64	111.25
16500	144.37	138.01	133.02	127.35	121.07	117.19	114.73
17000	148.74	142.19	137.05	131.21	124.74	120.74	118.20
17500	153.12	146.38	141.08	135.07	128.41	124.30	121.68
18000	157.49	150.56	145.11	138.93	132.08	127.85	125.16
18500	161.87	154.74	149.14	142.79	135.75	131.40	128.63
19000	166.24	158.92	153.17	146.65	139.42	134.95	132.11
19500	170.62	163.11	157.20	150.50	143.08	138.50	135.59
20000	174.99	167.29	161.24	154.36	146.75	142.05	139.06
20500	179.37	171.47	165.27	158.22	150.42	145.60	142.54
21000	183.74	175.65	169.30	162.08	154.09	149.15	146.02
21500	188.12	179.83	173.33	165.94	157.76	152.71	149.49
22000	192.49	184.02	177.36	169.80	161.43	156.26	152.97
22500	196.87	188.20	181.39	173.66	165.10	159.81	156.45
23000	201.24	192.38	185.42	177.52	168.77	163.36	159.92
23500	205.62	196.56	189.45	181.38	172.43	166.91	163.40
24000	209.99	200.75	193.48	185.24	176.10	170.46	166.87
24500	214.37	204.93	197.51	189.09	179.77	174.01	170.35
25000	218.74	209.11	201.54	192.95	183.44	177.57	173.83
26000	227.49	217.47	209.61	200.67	190.78	184.67	180.78
27000	236.24	225.84	217.67	208.39	198.12	191.77	187.73
28000	244.99	234.20	225.73	216.11	205.45	198.87	194.69
29000	253.74	242.57	233.79	223.83	212.79	205.98	201.64
30000	262.49	250.93	241.85	231.54	220.13	213.08	208.59
35000	306.24	292.75	282.16	270.14	256.82	248.59	243.36
40000	349.99	334.58	322.47	308.73	293.51	284.10	278.12

Let us calculate the MIF on Freeman as I did when I bought it. Net-in-Hand balance sheet for Freeman Property at the time I bought it:

Total Yearly Rents $5,880.00

Payouts:
Taxes .... $ 721.00
Fuel (unheated)
Other utilities supplied by owner (none)
Janitor cost (none)
Furniture repairs (none)
Insurance 113.00
Water 60.00
Total Annual Mortgage payments includ-
ing interest and principal on first mort-
gage, $24,000 at 4% 20 year basis 1,752.48
on 2nd mortgage $3,000, 4% 10 years   364.56
Total Payouts $3,011.04

Deduct Payouts from total rents. Balance is Net in $3,011.04
Hand $2,868.96

This indicated that I would have $2,868.96 left in hand each year out of which I must bear repairs and vacancies. Since rents were then controlled at low figures, I did not fear vacancies. According to the rent-control law, if a tenant vacated, the rent ceiling on that apartment no longer applied, and I was free to charge what I wished. The tenants knew well they were getting a bargain and asked for almost nothing by way of repairs except those which were absolutely required. Any future loss I would have to bear in these two categories was offset by the increases in rents that I was certain to obtain.

At this time we should observe another source of "silent profit" that this and other buildings make for the owner. We call it Principal Reduction. It refers to the regular reduction of the balance due on the mortgage which is contained *within* the above mentioned payments on mortgages.

Note that the first mortgage in the amount of $24,000 would

be automatically wiped out in 20 years, and the second mortgage of $3000 in 10 years. Thus, in effect, the building was be-
ing bought for me but it was being paid for *by the tenants.* That
figures out:

$24,000 paid off in 20 years . . . . average per year	$1,200
3,000 paid off in 10 years. . . . average per year	300
Total Average Gain By Me Per Year *Besides Net in Hand*	$1,500

If you will compare this with the $3000 I invested, you will
see that it means that in addition to the 100 per cent or so per
year I was making *in hand,* I was clearing another 50 per cent
or so per year in the bank.

And there's more—much more. What a business!

But, you may say, that was in the mid-forties. What about
now? The answer is that the figures are even better, much
better, today. We will see in the later chapter on "How To Sell
Them" that although taxes and other expenses rose in the next
ten years, rents rose even more, leaving a much greater net, and
enabling me to sell this property for $60,000! And mark you,
the buyer got a good buy!

Before we move on to apply the Balance Sheet for Net-in-
Hand to No. 16 property, we should pause and note the
strikingly high net in hand return that Freeman showed in
comparison to the amount I invested. My total investment was
only $3000. *In each year I held the property I cleared more
than that above all payments.*

The emphasis that I wish to make at this point is on the
remarkable balance shown in hand on a true Aunt Toby—one
where you do not furnish heat to the tenants. Let us apply the
Net-in-Hand Balance sheet to No. 16, a heated property, as it
presented itself when I bought it. Please do not let the low
interest rates, fuel costs, nor taxes disturb your judgment. These
were the current rates at the time. When we later discuss the
selling of these properties we shall see how the rising costs
were more than offset by the rising income.

Net-in-Hand Balance Sheet for No. 16

Total Yearly Rents $6,000.00

Payouts
   Taxes .... $ 807.00
   Fuel 715.00
   Other Utilities Supplied; Electricity for
      lighting halls and oilburner 71.00
   Janitor cost 180.00
   Furniture repairs, etc. (none) ....   —
   Insurance 74.00
   Water 88.00
   Mortgage payments; on first mortgage
      $19,000 @ 4½% on 20 year basis 1,442.52

   Total Payouts $3,377.52

   Deduct from rents. Balance is Net-in-Hand $2.622.48

That meant a return on my investment of some 44% per year.
Besides, it must be remembered that I was being enriched each
year on an average of $950 which was being paid off on my
mortgage—*by the tenants!* As in the Freeman property, I did
not fear vacancies—I welcomed them. Any apartment that became vacant, even though vacant a month or two, would
soon be producing so much more rent than the previous tenant
had paid that it would not only cover the lost rent but would
put the building on a more profitable basis.

I also held out the hope that rent controls would soon be
removed and I could set the rents at reasonable levels commensurate with the quality of the apartments and the services
They were decontrolled about six months after I sold the
building. By that time, the permitted rent ceiling increases and
other rules had raised the income to approximately $7000. We
will discuss this under How To Sell Them.

16

BEFORE THE OFFER

You have applied the basic tests of Location, Modesty of Rents, and where possible, Self-heat. The building has passed these tests and next you applied the Value Formula. Here you learned how much the property was worth. This established a limit, with some variance permitted, of how much you could afford to pay for the property. Your final test of the Net-in-Hand Balance Sheet told you how much you could clear if you bought the property *under given terms*. That is, if you paid a certain amount down and obtained financing for the balance. There are several preliminary points you should understand before framing a definite offer.

The matter of flexibility is one which your MIF will determine for you. If a property is one on which the MIF is attractive, do not be afraid to bend a little. If you will have to pay 5 to 10 per cent more for it than you originally offered, still staying close to the limit set by the Value Formula, you are free to do so, *providing* the higher price, when you apply the MIF test, shows that you will still clear 25 per cent or more per year on the amount you invested in cash.

The other test will guide you in the decision to pay a little more. For instance, when the location is "tops"—or the property is in fine "kept up" condition, or the tenants have occupied for 20 years or more, these are extra-desirable features that sweeten the attractiveness of the investment. Where the purchase has passed the tests with flying colors, and will leave you a good MIF, a thousand dollars or so on the purchase price makes little difference. That thousand is going to be paid off by the tenants anyway!

On the other hand, you should not let external and unrelated urges distort your view of the business. In this regard I have seen a few dangerous and personal feelings of weakness undermine the entire project. The first was hurry.

In their anxiety to 'get going' some students have allowed their impatience to blind, or color, their reason. It is quite understandable that, once you have learned the know-how of this business through this book, and you know precisely how to proceed with fearless confidence, you may have some impatience to see your project under way. But this should never be permitted to hurry you into buying. Many students have phoned me to say, substantially, "I've been advertising for over a month now, and have seen a lot of junk, but I haven't seen anything yet that I'd even consider, except this one. It doesn't *quite* meet our standards but I feel that I'd like to get going, so I guess I'll buy it." A serious mistake.

Ed R., whom I mentioned earlier, was anxious too, at the start. When he had been looking around for some five or six weeks he became impatient and had reached a point where he was *too* willing to compromise his standards and tests. I protested, but he insisted it was worth it to get started even if he just got the experience out of the deal with little profit. Discouraged with the seeming lack of availabilities in his home city, Brockton, he bought a four family Aunt Toby in Quincy, Mass., a city nearby. Later he bought a three-family. When things started to click in Brockton, where he had begun to think there "just aren't any," he unloaded both Quincy properties at a profit, having learned, as you will, how to straighten them out and sell them. Now he concentrated on his home town. Within two years, his problem was not *finding* them—it was *absorbing* them as fast as they became available! Every one was in Brockton. He now saw that he hadn't scratched the surface of the supply. At this writing he has some seventy-six units.

Another frequent cause of trouble is the human weakness of a person who just plain "likes" the property. Often it is a handsome looking building. Of course, the basic error here is in the student permitting *his* attraction to come into the picture instead of the attraction he should concentrate on—that of the prospective tenant. We must remember that WE are not going to have to like it as a home, nor live in it. We MUST look through the eyes of the workingman whom we hope to attract as tenant and use his standards.

Failure to do this may lead to blinding ourselves to cold hard facts. Let us never forget what a wise and successful realty investor indirectly taught me. I knew his son and talked with him about his father's adventures in real estate. He had been very successful and had capsuled the key to success to his son thus, "Never forget that we are in the *arithmetic* business first, and very incidentally, in the real estate business." He was right. This remark embodied the key to his success in real estate. Luckily, our business is one which can almost entirely be governed by simple arithmetic. We live by it. And there is a fine secure feeling about it. Unlike the stock investor, who *cannot* calculate the future of a stock, we CAN, with 98 per cent certainty.

Of all the students whom I have trained and who have used their training to make their million, I would have classified Arthur C. as the one least likely to permit his heart to blind and over-rule his arithmetic. After all, he is an Armenian and he has suffered much. He has seen and felt poverty we could never imagine possible. People around him, those not slaughtered, tried to keep alive by boiling grass. He was the most realistic man I ever met. I was amazed when *he* turned out to be the only student who weakened on this point. Here is what happened.

For years I had been holding forth on the arithmetic upon

which we rely to determine the desirability of a parcel of property. Arthur well knew that I had held up as a horrible example the confiscatory tax rate in the City of Boston. I divulge no secret here when I say this, since it has been publicly announced and proved many times, both in the trade publications and in such journals as the *Saturday Evening Post* and other lay magazines and newspapers.

For examples, I had pointed out uncontrovertible evidence adduced by recent events in that city. A few years ago, the tax burden was so heavy that many of the owners lost or abandoned their properties to be vandalized and finally torn down or just permitted to rot, and ruin an entire neighborhood. Soon only 80 per cent of the real estate in Boston was paying taxes at all. And these were attempting to pay all the "costs" (some debated) of running 100 per cent of the city. Naturally the weaker ones buckled under the burden, and soon only 70 per cent of the real estate was paying taxes. And the budget *rose*. Of course, before long those among the 60 per cent who could not carry the added burden now fell by the wayside, and the entire load was dumped on the shoulders of the remaining taxpayers. Not only that, the budget was increased again and again. A sizable percentage of the real estate, distress and voluntary, was sold to non-taxable buyers in the course of these years. This does not help the situation either. As I write this in 1973, some 50 per cent or less of the real estate in the City of Boston pays taxes at all! Even the blind can see the handwriting on that wall. Today the tax rate for Boston is well over $180 per $1000 of assessed value. That assessed value is stoutly defended as being 66 per cent of the realistic true market value of the property.

Among some examples I always cite Mr. D's experience. He bought a building in Boston for $26,000. The current tax bill assessment was $22,000. The next year he was billed at $52,000 and there was little he could really do about it. Recently a building on Washington Street in Boston became overburdened and had to be auctioned off. Now we must bear in mind, that this part of Washington Street is comparable to Times Square in New York as the AAA1 location for business in Boston. And it is well established that there is always a buyer for this type of location, particularly among the investment trusts and the like. They make a practice of diversification of area in their investment portfolios, and tend to buy choice spots in each of the leading cities. Likewise insurance companies, et cetera.

This building was put on the block. It had been assessed at $650,000 for tax purposes. That, reduced to simple truths, was a postulation that the property was worth $1,000,000. By all odds,if this were true, there should have been many bidders willing to offer a million, and more.

The building was sold to the highest bidder for $300,000.

Recently the *Herald Traveler,* one of the two leading newspapers in Boston, moved out of its intown building and built a new plant in a suburb. Their old building was assessed at $2,500,000 and this represented a claimed market value of roughly $4,000,000. The biggest price they could obtain—and there was NO forced sale or distress involved—was $1,250,000. It was sold for that.

In my lectures I pointed out other statistics such as the fact that the Boston taxpayer pays an average of *twice* as much out of his gross income as the national average, and other such concrete arguments. So I was more than a little surprised to have Arthur C. phone me one day and somewhat sheepishly announce that he had just bought a building in Boston. He had pointedly *not* asked me about it first, but this was not in itself remarkable, since he already had his million and had long since reached a point where the simple application of the Value Formula and the MIF was all the guide he needed. "I knew you wouldn't approve, Bob, but—I bought it." Of course, I congratulated him, and wished him luck, but I fear he sensed the banality of my trite response. I asked, "Arthur, what made you do it? You know what you are supposed to do. You know your arithmetic. How come?"

His answer was the one I *least* expected from him. "Bob—I

just liked it. It's so clean, and—and—you stand across the street and look at it and you've got to fall in love with it."

Perhaps Arthur had some secret longing to possess something more appetizing to his vanity than a long succession of Aunt Tobys (which had made him a million.) But he had made a cardinal *business* error, and he knew it.

A year later he phoned me. He was in a "tizzy" as the New Englanders call it.

"Bob, Bob, what am I going to do? I just got my tax bill!"

I replied, "What's the matter with it?"

"It's—it's—awful!"

"What do you mean, awful?" I asked, as if I didn't know.

"Why, listen, Bob, when I get through paying this tax bill, I am not getting *one nickel* out of that building. I'm operating it entirely for the City of Boston."

I wasn't particularly worried about Arthur. He wouldn't starve. I gagged, "Well, Arthur, if you don't like the building, why don't you sell it?"

"You know dang well why I don't sell it," he snapped. "I CAN'T sell it. Anyone I'd show it to, would soon ask how much are the taxes, figure it out, and goodbye."

"Well, Arthur, I have some good news for you. You've just been awarded a very desirable appointment. I hereby appoint you, for *life*, official janitor of the building, to work for a dollar a year."

"Oh, Bob," he wailed, "you're no help."

The lesson to be learned by Arthur's experience is clear. We can never afford to ignore the message that our arithmetic gives.

Before we even start to frame our offer, we must honestly decide whether the building has passed the tests. It must not matter that:

We'd like to live there ourselves, or would not.

It's a very low price—a "bargain." We rely on our own arithmetic.

It's an attractive parcel.

We are in a hurry to get along.

We want experience.

The seller is in distress. Or the property is being auctioned.

Or any other consideration, such as nearness to our home, et cetera.

17

FRAMING THE OFFER

To frame our offer is simple. Let us say this is a typical Aunt Toby, a fine first-try example. Here are its facts. It is a wooden three-decker. (But the tests and results work out just as clearly and simply if it is a four-apartment duplex in California or a five-unit row of singles in Philadelphia.)

Good location
Self heat by tenants
Rents modest—$125 per flat per month
Taxes are $800 per year (typical proportionate Norm in U.S.)

It takes but a few minutes to apply the Value Formula. We need only use those lines in the Formula that apply here.
Value Formula for 38 X St.

Value Formula for 38 X St.

Step 1. Find the Annual Working Income:
Gross Yearly Rents $4,500.00
Less Taxes 800.00
Annual Working Income (AWI) .... $ 3,700.00

Step 2. List Above-Normal Expenses and Loss Factors:
Mortgage Interest above 8% (none)
Wood Exterior (it is) 10% of AWI 370.00
Deduction for Location Good—5% of AWI 185.00

Step 3. Add items in Step 2 and enter here 555.00

110

Step 4. Deduct Total from AWI
Balance is Primary Adjusted Income enter
in Box PAI
Section 11 Addition of Extra Profit Factors ..   Box PAI
$ 3,145.00

Step 5. List Extra Profit Factors
Any mortgage saving *under* 8% (None)
Parking, if available 5% of AWI 185.00
If all electric bills are paid by tenants 2% of
AWI 74.00

Step 6. Add extra profit factors to PAI. This is FINAL
Adjusted Income—enter here .... $ 3,404.00

Step 7. Multiply Final Adjusted Income by 6⅔%. This
is Gross Value—enter here $22,693.00

Step 8. Deduct cost of needed repairs (none)

Step 9. Fair Market Value of Property $22,693.00

This Value Formula has shown that our general limit is
$22,700. There is a present mortgage of $15,000 at 8 per cent
for a 20-year term. The payments for interest and principal are
$1,505.64 per year ($125.47 per month), plus taxes of $800
which are commonly deposited in the bank by installments
together with monthly mortgage payment, in preparation for
the payment of the bill, when it is rendered by the city. Here
is the MIF we would live with if we offered $19,000 with
$4,000 down, and buyer to assume the old mortgage.

Total yearly rents $4500.00
Payouts:
Taxes .... $ 800.00
Mortgage Payments 1505.64
Water 100.00
Insurance 110.00
Total Payouts (including principal) 2515.64
Leaving Net-in-Hand for vacancies and repairs $1984.36

If we made this offer, and it was accepted, we would have
a generous margin *in hand* each year *over and above* the 33⅓
per cent return in hand of our cash investment, with which to
bear temporary losses such as repairs and vacancies. And we

will learn later in this book how to hold *those* down to a tiny minimum. If we extracted our 33⅓ per cent of invested amount —$1,333—we would have $650 besides with which to cover these occasional expenditures, an amount far exceeding any normal or even rare loss.

Let us take the same example, for purposes of variety, with an existing $7000 mortgage that was written at 7 percent on a 20-year basis. This is a set of facts you will encounter more frequently than the first example. Naturally, we would like to enjoy the 7 per cent interest rate for the years to come. So we try to buy it with the same $4,000 down and we pay the balance by:

Assuming the old mortgage of $7,000 (originally $10,000)
Giving a new second mortgage at 8% (and even 10% for $8000 on a 10 year basis.

Let us see what the MIF would be

Total Yearly Rents		$4500.00
Payouts:		
Taxes	$ 800.00	
1st mortgage payments $77.53 per mo. or	930.36	
2nd mortgage payments $97.06 per mo. or	1164.72	
Water	100.00	
Insurance	110.00	3105.08
Net-in-Hand for vacancies and repairs MIF		$1394.92

Still not bad, is it? Particularly when you take into account that under this plan you (out of the tenants' pockets) are paying off mortgages and enriching yourself thereby $1230 per year in addition.

Let us see how our MIF would stand up if we paid the limit, $22,700. This we would *not* do unless we could get attractive financing. You will find two typical situations as to financing, old financing and new financing. We will consider the results under both of them.

Suppose there exists a $9000, (originally $12,000) 6 per cent mortgage for 20 years. You wish to know how your MIF would look if you paid $22,700, with $4,000 down, assumed the existing 1st mortgage and gave a new second mortgage to the seller at 8 per cent, 10 years for $9,700.

Total Yearly Rents $4500.00

    Payouts:
      Taxes .... $ 800.00
      1st mortgage payments, $85.97 per mo. or   1031.64
      2nd mortgage payments, $38.86 per mo. or   1412.28
      Water 100.00
      Insurance 110.00

    Total payouts 3453.92

Leaving Net-in-Hand (MIF) for vacancies and repairs $1046.08

Observe that we have an MIF that leaves us our 25 per cent of our investment in hand plus a fat safe amount for margin, plus the annual gain we enjoy thru principal payments of $1533 per year, average.

Note that in this extreme example we have taken the position that rents will not stand increase and that we are paying top price for the property. As a final variation, let us do the MIF on this parcel under the conditions called "new financing." This means that the seller has little or no mortgage outstanding for us to take over and we must completely refinance. In general, you will find that the local Building-and-Loan, Co-operative bank, or Federal Savings and Loan will quote terms to you thus:

Bank will lend 80 per cent of the purchase price, providing you do not have a bad credit background (no bank wants troublesome collection headaches) and you will have to pay the remaining 20 per cent of the purchase price in cash, providing you cannot convince the seller to take *part* of that 20 per cent by way of 2nd mortgage. Often you will be able to arrange this.

Later in this book, when you learn the tax benefits that the seller gains by selling for low down payments and taking the mortgage himself, you will be able to show him why it is far more to his advantage to finance it for you. But for our extreme case, let us assume the seller has another need for his money, or for any other reason, you must buy it with completely new financing, at $22,000.

You will find it very effective and helpful in proposing the loan, to have with you a typed, neat copy of the MIF sheet, and leave it with the Mortgage Officer. Also, if you wish, a copy of the Value Formula may impress him and show that you have authoritatively arrived at the offer figure, rather than just guessed at it. Here is how your MIF will look under these extreme conditions:

Total Yearly Rents $4500.00

Payouts:
Taxes .... $ 800.00
1st Mortgage payts at 8%, 20 years $18,000   1806.72
Water 100.00
Insurance 110.00
Total Payouts 2816.72

Leaving, on $2800 investment, in hand for vacancies and
repairs $1683.28

Note that in this "top-price, worst-terms" example, you still have 25% of your investment in hand, or $1000 plus $683 extra to care for vacancies and repairs. However, if you were forced to pay a prohibitive tax on the property, say $1600 instead of $800, your MIF would be seriously slashed. Of course the Value Formula would never permit you to pay $22,000 for it if the taxes were $1600, anyway.

In keeping with our objective, which is to acquire as much property as possible with our limited bankroll, and let *the property* (or tenants) pay for itself, rather than have it come out of our pockets, we try hard for low down payments. This will result in our getting our investment out in two, three or four years and we are enabled to buy more. Pursuant to this, it is helpful to point out to the seller that the cash he receives does not grow by itself. It must be invested. And where could he invest it and get 8 per cent true interest with perfect safety? Or 9 per cent?

If your circumstances are like most, and you need to stretch your savings over as many properties as possible, you will need to point out these advantages to convince the seller who has placed his property on the market with the intention of getting his cash. We will discuss the other arguments you can use in the chapter on Taxes, but one idea to stress is, "With the 2nd mortgage, you have no further headaches. Your money, interest and principal, comes to you in the mail regularly and dependably. You are the bank. You do not have to concern yourself with renting, repairs, complaints—nothing. You just get a steady *annuity* with no bother or risk."

Then he may protest, "But I still remain liable on the old first mortgage. If you don't pay it, I'm responsible." Your comeback is, "I know you don't want the property back, but what chance is there of that? After all you have my down payment of $4000. Then you will have the payments I make to you from this point on. In addition you have the benefit of the amounts I will have paid off on the first mortgage. If I should die or go broke, you will *gain!* You get the property back, you are several thousand dollars to the good, and you can sell it again. You are in a solid position either way." Sometimes I have found a seller still concerned and have overcome his fears by this one.

"You are worried as to whether I will keep up the payments on the first mortgage? OK, here's what we'll do. I will give you a note stating that I will send you, each month, besides the payment on the second mortgage, a check made out to the first mortgagee-bank for that payment. I will enclose the payment book and an envelope to the bank, and you can check for yourself that it has been paid by forwarding it yourself. This will continue for five years. After that, I know you will not be worried."

In extreme cases, I have found this one effective.

"You say you are concerned with the possibility that I will not keep up the payments and that you may have to foreclose, at some expense to you. Here is what I will do. We will make a contract and I will agree to place a signed, sealed and acknowledged deed in *your* lawyer's hands, in escrow (in trust, as a stakeholder), and I will sign that I will not deed nor mortgage the property to anyone else for the five years. If I should fail to make a payment, you can wipe me out *without any expense or bother*. You just record the deed and you have my down payment, my payments to you and the bank, *and* the property."

Another seemingly minor point you should remember about making your offer concerns the amount to be posted with the offer. Of course, no offer is worth the paper it is written on, in the eyes of the seller, unless it is accompanied by cash or a check, preferably certified. Strangely enough, this point has been ignored by most people in my experience, and in many cases, as I have seen repeatedly demonstrated, it meant the difference between success and failure, acceptance or rejection. I suppose it is because people naturally tend to part with as little money as possible and then postpone parting with as much of it as possible, as long as possible.

You should remember that the seller, too, is subject to this habit. *Use* his aversion to parting with money, to your advantage. That is why I always recommend placing a deposit of $1000, by bank cashier's check, with every offer, as a minimum, and where convenient, more. The seller has certain weaknesses and we should use them in making our offer. One of them is the natural unwillingness to part with $1000. If he contemplates returning the deposit, he (or his wife) will recall the old "bird-in-the-hand" bit. It is my experience and conviction that NO seller ever returns a deposit without at least wondering whether he is doing the right thing, and whether he may one day regret it.

We have all been told as children that if we "throw away bread" we will "one day hunger for it." Nobody can read the future. "Sure," the seller may ponder, "I *think* I will get more, but who knows? What went up can come down. The property cost me much less and I've had a fine profit out of it—up to now. This offer gives me a good selling profit. I might use that money to buy much bigger parcels. What might happen in the future— no one knows. But this, this $1000 is positive!"

There is no danger in attaching the cashier's check for $1000 to your offer, provided you word it as you should. Every contingency that I have ever seen or heard of, has been covered so that you cannot lose it. Either the deal goes through as you set it out, or the deposit must be returned within three days. The only exception to this three-day deadline occurs where the seller is out of the state or country, or where the property is owned by an estate. But even here, your money will only be tied up for a week or two at most, if the offer is rejected.

Here is the form of offer that has been used for almost all the transactions in which I or my clients and students have bought. Not all offers were accepted, but in no case did the making of the offer cause complications, court action or difficulty in getting the deposit back if it was rejected.

When you make your offer relying upon obtaining a new mortgage, you use the term contained in (1) and strike out (2).

Where your offer is on the basis that you are going to assume the old first mortgage, fill in (2) and strike out (1). This protects you if it should transpire that the bank, for any reason, will not give the loan and provides that if so, you are to receive a refund of the deposit and be relieved of further obligation in the matter.

If you are going to pay all cash, you should strike out both (1) and (2).

Most of the examples cited here and certainly some 90 per cent of the purchases that my graduates have made in past years, required $3000 or less in cash. As you progress in the business your cash reserves will accumulate as mine did. Then, of course, you will have a broader field of acquisition because you will be able to muster the cash needed. Until then, I assume you are the average beginner with a small amount of capital.

OFFER

DATE: .... 19....

The undersigned BUYER offers to BUY the Real Estate Situated at

No. .... St., ... State ....

Total Price .... $ ....

Deposit herewith .... $ ....

Balance due SELLER at passing of papers $ ....

Cash to be paid by BUYER at passing of papers

(over and above mortgage loan if any) .. $ .. ..

(1) This Agreement is subject to the BUYER obtaining a new first mortgage for

$ .... at ....% for .... years.

(2) The balance of the purchase price to be paid by assuming the present first mortgage of $ .... to be adjusted to the balance at the time of passing.

Papers and the deed to be passed on .... 19 ....

The SELLER to give the BUYER possession of ....

.... on .... 19 ....

The SELLER to pay a regular commission of .... % as per

.... rates to ...., Broker. SELLER to give a good and marketable title by quitclaim deed, subject to easements and restrictions of record, and may use part of the purchase money to pay existing encumbrances. Should the property be damaged by fire before the passing of papers, the buyer has the option to withdraw and receive his deposit. If BUYER defaults he waives claim to the deposit above which becomes the property of the SELLER and BROKER, equally, as liquidated damages. Interest, Rents, Fuel, Taxes, to be adjusted as of the date of passing. All regular fixtures to pass with sale.

....

....:....

....

This offer to be accepted within .... days of date or deposit returned and offeror discharged.

                              Buyer: ....(Seal)

              Buyer's wife: (husband) ....(Seal)

ACCEPTED: .... 19 ....

Seller: ....(Seal)

Seller's wife: (husband) ....(Seal)

(Broker) ....(Seal)

Order these forms direct from:
(c) REALFORMS Box 1, Brookline, Mass. 02146 Form #0
USE IN TRIPLICATE WITH BALL POINT PEN

To familiarize ourselves with the process of making the offer, let us fill one out for a model Aunt Toby, the one we set out the facts for at the beginning of this chapter. (Page 110 top).

The terms of our offer will use (2) for the balance so that we can omit (1).

OFFER

DATE: .... *March 5* 19.*60*..

The undersigned BUYER offers to BUY the Real Estate Situated at

No. *38 Oak* St., *Brookline* State *Mass.*

Total Price .... $ *22,000.00*

Deposit herewith .... $ *1,000.00*

Balance due SELLER at passing of papers $ *3,000 plus*

2nd mortgage as described below

Cash to be paid by BUYER at passing of papers
(over and above mortgage loan if any) .. $ *3,000*

(1) This Agreement is subject to the BUYER obtaining a new first mortgage for

$ .... at ....% for .... years.

(2) The balance of the purchase price to be paid by assuming the present first mortgage of $ *15,000.00* to be adjusted to the balance at the time of passing.

Papers and the deed to be passed on ..... *April 5* 19 *73*

The SELLER to give the BUYER possession of ....

.... on .... 19 ....

The SELLER to pay a regular commission of .....5..... % as per

........*agreement*........ to ......*John Agent*......, Broker.

SELLER to give a good and marketable title by quitclaim deed, subject to easements and restrictions of record, and may use part of the purchase money to pay existing encumbrances. Should the property be damaged by fire before the passing of papers, the buyer has the option to withdraw and receive his deposit. If BUYER defaults he waives claim to the deposit above which becomes the property of the SELLER and BROKER, equally, as liquidated damages. Interest, Rents, Fuel, Taxes, to be adjusted as of the date of passing. All regular fixtures to pass with sale. Seller to take back a 2nd mortgage for 10 years at 8% with payments monthly of $48.53 inclusive of interest and principal.

....

....

....

This offer to be accepted within .....*three*..... days of date or deposit returned and offeror discharged.

Buyer: .....*Bill Buyer*..... .(Seal)

Buyer's wife: (husband) ....(Seal)

ACCEPTED: .... 19 ....

Seller: ....(Seal)

Seller's wife: (husband) ....(Seal)

(Broker) ....(Seal)

Order these forms direct from:
(*c*) REALFORMS Box 1, Brookline, Mass. 02146 Form #0

USE IN TRIPLICATE WITH BALL POINT PEN

18

THE OFFER

It may be best to make your offer several times, each time raising it a little and then if not accepted, to "give it a rest." Let the seller think you are finished, and it also helps to implant the hint that you are wavering between his property and another. Now that he has turned down your offer you have washed your hands of his deal and are going ahead with "the rival." Of course it does not do to send in a higher offer immediately after rejection of an earlier one. That will soon give the seller the hint that if he holds out long enough he will get top price.

I have found that spacing should be a minimum of ten days between the first and second offers and two weeks between any subsequent ones. In no case is it wise to make more than three or four. If you have been rejected three or four times, and still feel you want this building badly enough to hurry its purchase, it is better to sit down and talk with the owner face to face and hash out what is the final bottom price. Then you take it or walk away.

An old friend, Peter Turchon, who owns the country's biggest home-remodeling company and buys and sells an average of 500 homes a year, says, "We cannot afford to pay for a man's love for the property. We must buy it for what it is worth. We cannot afford heart-balm on top of the price."

It is not difficult to understand how many owners have

heard rumors, many false, of how this seller or that got a big price for his property, and as a result have put an unrealistically high price on their buildings. Ofter this is because the owner has worked on it with his own hands, nursed it, fixed it, cleaned it, painted it. It is his baby. But it cannot be yours. You are buying income-producing merchandise and that's all.

Perhaps the most profitable state of mind the buyer should maintain is, "There are plenty of properties. If I do not buy this one, there will be dozens more and better ones. *I can wait.*" And that is the truth.

If the property is a choice piece, that is, if the MIF and Value Formula say yes at (let us say) $22,000, you can proceed to $21,000 and *stop there*. The figure of $22,000 must come from *him*. If necessary, ask him definitely and finally, what his bottom price is, and don't accept too quickly even if he mentions $22,000. Take a few days to "think about it" and offer to split before you accept. I stress this procedure because I have found that if you accept the $22,000 figure quickly you make the seller back off and wonder whether he could not have gotten more. Since he has as yet signed nothing, you may find that he stalls on the signing and later comes back with, "My wife won't let me sell under $24,000. That's final."

Some examples in this regard are outstanding in my experience and may assist you in this matter of offers. In the course of counseling and guiding students and friends, I have encountered these situations.

A student comes to me with the facts on a property and raves about the location and the other choice features of it. The Value Formula says $30,000. Says the student, "He's asking $23,000 and I offered him $20,000. If he'd come down just $1,000 I'd grab it." The student is a victim of a habit. He *cannot* ever bring himself to pay what is asked *for anything*. If he cannot beat the seller down, he simply cannot bring himself to buy. I answer him in five words. "Stop fooling around. Buy it."

PRECAUTIONS IN THE OFFER

When making the offer, be sure to fill out the part that specifies that unless you get certain financing, on specific terms, you get your deposit back and all parties are discharged from all obligations.

There are a few things that you should carefully set out on your offer to be sure you get what you should with the property and that it is paid for, and that you DO NOT get what you shouldn't. Any furniture, refrigerators, rugs, et cetera, that will go with the property should be identified and listed in the offer as passing with the building and your lawyer will see that you are protected at the time of passing papers, against the danger of existing claims, liens, et cetera, on the items.

It is well to incorporate in the offer, since it becomes your agreement after both have signed, what leases, if any, exist. You may encounter a case where the owner has given a relative a ten-year lease on an apartment for a very low rent and you may be forced to respect it.

If your state has rent controls, it would be necessary that the apartments be identified and the seller should warrant what the rents being collected are and that they are in accordance with legal rent ceilings.

These things will be checked later by your lawyer when he consummates the deal at passing papers, but he cannot hold the seller to anything that is not in the written agreement, or contract, since this is presumed to contain within its four corners, *all* the terms and representations that the parties have made.

If there is any possibility that the building was ever converted, as from one-family to three-family, it is also provident that you incorporate in the offer the words:

"Seller warrants that the building is legally a three-family building in accordance with the building and zoning laws of the city and state." Buyer to have a termite inspection at his expense and unless the report is satisfactory to buyer, deposit to be returned and all parties discharged.

19

AFTER ACCEPTANCE

When the seller signs and dates his acceptance at the bottom of our offer form, we are ready to put certain machinery into motion in preparation for taking over. Our first call is to the insurance agent.

When people buy real estate, they are notoriously neglectful of certain highly dangerous situations that exist. One of the most glaring is that of insurance. Often I have seen this to be so in transactions even though the buyer is represented by competent counsel. This is especially true where the buyer delays seeking out his counsel until the passing of papers, or leaves it to the bank lawyer to represent his interests at the passing. You should make contact with a *not too busy* lawyer who will be glad to get *all* your business and who is not too proud to accept suggestions from you as to some precautions and procedures you will have learned here. Have him represent you, and have him look over your offer before you present it, if you can.

If he is your lawyer, he has only one master to serve, unlike those cases wherein the bank lawyer acts for two or more parties. Your lawyer will have things to do in your behalf that are much better done by one who is not too busy to find time to do them thoroughly and who is willing to take the pains for his fee.

It is precisely because it is a dangerous practice to transfer insurance that I have omitted the customary reference to this point in the offer. Ordinarily the seller remains covered against loss until he either sells the property or until *the company assents* to a transfer of the policy. In other words, when you sit down to pass papers and the deed, and the seller signs an assignment of his policy to you, and you pay him proportionately, there is not the faintest obligation on the company to honor that assignment until its authorized representative has assented to and signed the transfer. If you are to be protected against the very serious danger of a crippling lawsuit, you must take other precautionary measures that seem to be customary in legal practices in my experience.

To put it bluntly, you must be protected against public liability from the moment you take title. This can only be accomplished by one of two means. One way is to have the insurance transfers drawn a week or so before the passing of papers, and have them effective as of the time of passing title, have them signed by the seller and then assented to by an authorized representative of the insurance company. The other method is usually a little more costly in that you will pay more for the insurance than if you took over the old policy. This means placing a new policy on the property before you take over, covering yourself as of the day before you take title. This may save you from loss only once in a lifetime, but that loss is so catastrophic as to merit your precautionary steps. My own experience demonstrates this.

I signed an agreement with Jim R. to sell me Pond Avenue on April 4. We were to pass papers on May 1. He was covered by a well-known company and one would think the company would never avail itself of a subterfuge to evade responsibility. But here is what happened.

The old liability policy would be transferred to me on May 1 but the assignment would then be forwarded to the company for assent as a routine matter, and might take a week or more. Between May 1, at 10 A.M., and perhaps May 10, there was nothing by way of any policy, contract or concent, signed by the insurance company, wherein they agreed to cover Bob Kent. Their contract was with Jim R. If a tenant or visitor should fall on a defective step, or in a darkened hallway, and sue me, I would be on my own.

Hence I called Ace Todd, my insurance man, and covered as of April 30. In the usual course of its business, Ace's company sent out an interviewer to check on the tenants of the building to be sure there were no professional suers in the building. The first floor tenant, a Mrs. V., would answer no questions as to her maiden name, et cetera, until the (dumb) insurance man told her the purpose of his call. He informed Mrs. V. that I was taking over on May 1 and that his company would be covering against Owner's Landlord and Tenants Liability. Mrs. V. answered the questions and the coverage was confirmed to me on April 25.

On May 1, I met with Jim R. and he signed an assignment of the policy he held with U Company to me. Then the assignment was forwarded to U Company's agent for the usual assent.

On May 2, Mrs. V's mother-in-law came to visit her and fell, she said, on a cracked step, injuring herself severely. I was served with the usual summons and writ. If things had turned out as badly in this case as they have often done in similar cases, I would have been wiped out. When I called U Company to ask them to cover, they informed me that their contract (the policy) was to protect Jim R., not me. Until they had signed the assent, accepting me as assured, they had no obligation to cover the loss *I* had suffered. Legally, of course, they were right.

By the way, Mrs. V., by her own acts spoiled her own case. She sent me the rent for May and enclosed a letter which she thought would strengthen her case. It said that *when she moved into the flat* she had noted the cracked step and had called Mr. R's attention to it but he had never fixed it. Under our laws, the tenant who knows of and accepts a condition like this is said to assent to it in the hiring and any damage resulting from it is not the responsibility of the owner. Any guest of the tenant or member of his family is bound by the same bar, and thus Mrs. V. and her mother-in-law got nothing.

There is another most vital insurance matter that should be attended to, before the passing. If there is an employee of any kind, part time or full time, you must cover for Workmen's Compensation Insurance so that you are covered from the day *before* you take over. If your state does not have a Workmen's Compensation law or its equivalent, you can and must place a policy that will cover you should the janitor be carrying a rubbish barrel up a cellar stairway and take a nasty fall, or be up on a ladder and tumble.

In this regard it is well to note a word of caution as to who is classified legally as an employee. Many owners are often misled by the fact that a part-time or "contract" janitor only comes in a few hours a week to do a few chores, and is not bound by any requirement to put in any given hours, nor is he under the direction or control of the owner. Yet that janitor will probably be deemed your legal employee if he is hurt, and you may have to pay important damages when the jury or Arbitration Board passes on the case. It has even been decided that the janitor was an employee in cases where it was proved that the work was contracted to a company who could send any of its men to do the work, even men whom the owner did not know.

It is immaterial that you pay the man for the work on a flat or monthly basis, and that you do not direct nor control his labors. Some states have declared him an employee in spite of this, on the premise that you "could have controlled him, had you so chosen."

A final word on this matter as to the usual maintenance companies that may be giving service or care to your building. Exterminators, window washers, cleaners, washroom service companies, floor waxers and the like come within this category. If there be any such companies servicing your building, you ARE concerned with the question of whether *the service company* has employee's compensation insurance!

Even though you do not hire the workman who comes to spray the bug-juice, or clean the windows, you can, in most states be held liable to his widow when the window washer makes his one allowed mistake from a high window. And *it is no help* to you that the window washing company has assured you (or even signed with you) that they will keep their help insured. It is your obligation to *see* the certificate of insurance that the company *says* it has. Otherwise you stand in danger of losing all if there is an accident. Remember, even a written contract between you and the contractor, guaranteeing to hold you harmless if an accident occurs, will avail you nothing. Nor will it help if you show the company's business stationery and business cards or phone book ads, warranting that the company is fully covered. You MUST see or hold the certificate. Nothing else will do.

The above warnings serve to emphasize again the freedom from care that is afforded us by owning Aunt Tobys.

Your final step in the pre-passing stage is the physical inspection of the building for any dangerous conditions that may exist in the halls, walks or common stairways. Loose banisters, frayed stairtreads, cracked steps, broken glass, absent handrails, papers or rubbish under stairs should be corrected. In those buildings where the custom, the letting, or the local laws require you to keep the stairs lighted, you will want to check that the lights are in order, and you may plan to install an inexpensive clock-switch to turn them on and off at pre-set times. Usually you will change the time setting in the clock twice a year, but beyond that they require no care or attention. It is notoriously dangerous to rely on memory, yours or the janitor's, to turn the lights on at the required time. Failing to do so may result in a serious lawsuit. In those cases where the custom is for the tenants to light their own halls, this entire responsibility is removed from your shoulders.

CHECKING THE HEAT

If you are to buy a heated building and pass papers in the fall or early fall, you will find it much better to check over the heat during the summer, even before you pass papers. It is much more difficult to effect full efficiency of the system and iron out all its bugs, when any interruption of the heat evokes complaint from the tenants.

If the building is one that is heated by the owner, fuel will be one of your biggest expenses, and there is much that you can do in this area to put the building on an efficient basis. Preliminary surveys of the heating system may be begun at this time. Since heat bills form such an important drain on the income of a building, not to mention how the heat situation is the source of complaint more than all other items combined, we can and should devote some attention to effecting economy, satisfaction of the tenants, and freedom from breakdown and trouble, particularly when it is most annoying—in zero weather.

Start with a visit to the oil supplier. Explain to him that you would like to continue to buy from him, but will expect prompt service and will want his best expert (or the boss himself) to look over the system. Since oil will be the most frequently encountered system, we will list the recommended check points for oil systems.

If the interior of the fire chamber in the heating boiler is thick with soot, this is both a serious loss factor and a clear indication of an inefficient system. Properly burned oil leaves little soot. The soot forms a coating on the inside of the heater and this insulates the surfaces *against* the absorption of the heat that the burner generates, letting it go up the chimney. The proper use of the heat is to pass it through the iron walls of the chamber to the water jacket, and thence to heat the building.

Sootiness is corrected in either of two ways. The burner nozzle and mixture should be adjusted to properly vaporize the oil for complete combustion. This will stop the further accumulation of excess soot, after the heater has been cleaned. Another and more permanent method is to change the burner for one of a new type which is *built* for and with, a device called a Shell Head. The word "built" is emphasized because it is inadvisable to change over a standard burner to the use of the Shell Head. Nor is it satisfactory in those cases where the burner manufacturer uses a standard burner and simply switches the fire head for a Shell. The burner *must* be built for the Shell Head to be fully effective in its purpose. This type of burner is so thorough in the revolutionary way it vaporizes the oil, that the oil is practically completely burned, and soot, which is the result of incomplete vaporization and combustion, is rarely formed.

A triple benefit results. The oil you buy is completely used instead of wasted. The heater absorbs the heat instead of repelling it and sending it up the chimney. And the breakdowns and repair bills are fewer.

It has been estimated that most breakdowns result from one single cause. That is inadequate filtration of the oil before it reaches the burner. When you consider that oil comes largely from desert-like soil, and contains fine sand and sludge, it is not surprising that any fine orifice through which it must pass will soon become clogged unless thorough filtration has been effected. Thousands of gallons must pass through some small filters in the burner and finally through a needle-size hole in the nozzle. It takes very little gunk or sand to plug the small filters or the nozzle.

After some study of the problem, I learned that ocean-going vessels that burned oil had met the same problem and had conquered it through repeated filtration. I decided that every drop of oil that entered my burners would get thorough and repeated filtering before it entered, and I installed two giant filters (called here AS no. 8), for each burner. One caught the sand and sludge just as the oil left the tank and the other was installed at the other end of the pipeline, just before the burner. Each filter had its core replaced every August. Winter breakdowns dropped to $\frac{1}{20}$ of their former number and burners lasted much longer, now that the grinding effect of the sand in the oil was eliminated. Pump parts in the burner and other important machinery that used to be worn away by the sand and grit now lasted indefinitely.

Controls are your next concern. These may affect your oil bill drastically. In the long run, an outdoor control, mounted in a shady spot, such as under a porch or eave, will save most oil, and still give the building its proper warm-up in the mornings and regulated heat during the day. This device makes allowances for such variants as sunny afternoons, bitterly cold nights requiring longer warmups before 7 A.M., et cetera, doing it all automatically. These controls often cost as much as $100 installed, however, and take some adjustment before they are completely right for your building and system. Indoor clock thermostats, often called Chronotherms are more popular because of the comparative ease of installation, adjustment and servicing, and cost only one-fourth as much as the outdoor type. These should be installed in the apartment or unit most remote from the heating system, on a wall that is *not* an outside wall, about eye level.

Of course, you will check carefully in the room where you mount the thermostat, against serious heat leaks. Upper sashes of windows that do not completely close, can cause the room temperature to fall so that the thermostat feels the need of heat almost continuously and your bills will soar.

It is well to check every window in the building in this regard and where needed, window cords or weather strips should be installed. In some buildings I have encountered such leaky, loose windows that the heat was entirely out of balance. In order to satisfy the third floors, the second and first floors had to be heated to 80 degrees or so. This was corrected by installing aluminum windows on the third floors. Thereafter, the thermostat became "satisfied" more easily and the lower floors were practically the same temperature as the third, with a nice saving in fuel and much added comfort.

By the way, it is almost common to find that the oil dealer extends a "discount" from the recommended standard price of fuel oil to those who request it. You may be asked to keep it mum, but there is no harm in trying. One cent off is the usual cut, and for a large-volume buyer, 1½ cents off may often be enjoyed. With No. 2 fuel oil this amounts to about 10 per cent —a substantial saving.

Note that it is always best, where possible, to use the same oil company as your supplier of fuel and for servicing the oil burner. This bars the common excuse by the service man that the "oil you're getting is bad" and the retort by the oil supplier that, "It's your service that's at fault."

20

AFTER TAKING TITLE

The usual thing is for new owners to acquire "new owner's disease" and you should steel yourself against it. This means that most folks who have just taken over their first or second building are inclined to give it *too much* attention. They seem to be unable to stay away from it, like a grandfather with his son's first-born. In the same spirit as the new grandpa, the new owner seems to stay awake nights dreaming up things he can spend for on his new baby. I have heard some rationalize when they felt this way by some such excuse as "I just can't stand it to have that unsightly back hall. *I must* re-do it."

Don't fall victim to the standard malady. In fact, as soon as the straightening out process of the building (not the tenants) is finished, you should confine your visits to three types. First, when it is necessary to show a prospective new tenant a flat. I have even avoided this by leaving the door unlocked and sending new tenants over to look around for themselves.

The second, and main category of visit is to look over the need for a repair and arrange things with the mechanic who will do it. This includes the careful inspection of the job when finished. Besides the two above, you need only stop by once a month or once every two months. Walk around the building, checking for broken windows, cellar windows particularly, and tour the front and rear halls and stairways for dangerous conditions.

EXTERIORS

Outer sidewalls vary from stucco in the Southwest and Southeast to shingles and clapboards in the Northeast. You will want the outer appearance to be respectable, and if it is shabby, you have made allowance in your Value Formula for the cost of bringing it up to the standard of *this* class of housing.

A really tattered or shabby exterior usually is best covered, rather than patched. In effect you give the building a new overcoat, and the primary objective in this is to have a neat appearance without having to maintain or repair the work endlessly. You will have no difficulty determining what is the best permanent outer covering for your section of the country. There are, however, a few methods that have never, in all my experience, been good investments.

Where paint is peeling, scaled, blistered or cracked, you should rigidly avoid repainting. At best you will get a year or so of good appearance, and then the blistering recurs. No painter I have ever met has been willing to correct this either, blaming the moisture in the wood, or some other cause. The fact is, he cannot guarantee such a surface against blistering or peeling. These buildings should be covered with a permanent sidewalling. The sidewalling should be nailed over as much of the walls as possible, covering the corners, trim and window facings and dormers, if any. Thus you will leave an absolute minimum of exterior wall exposed to the weather, to require periodic scraping and painting.

There are two common types of sidewalling used, and it is best to avoid the type known as asphalt shingles or panels. These are basically tarpaper with some coating and fine pebbles. They look very neat and attractive on a display board but are comparatively short-lived.

I have had fine results with the type called *asbestos* shingles. These are moulded of fireproof material and their color is through and through the shingle, rather than on the surface. They are rot-proof, permanent and act as a heat insulator. In some cases you can have your fire insurance premiums lowered after installing them.

Your choice of installer of sidewalls is important if not vital. Unfortunately, many unscrupulous people have gone into this business and their methods leave something to be desired. Some pay the salesman 30 or 40 per cent and more as selling commission. Many have no plant, stock, or workmen. They take your order, cash it at the bank, and then have the shingles delivered to your home from the distributor. They then hand the job to an independent installation crew at so much per 100 square feet. Of course it is to the crew's interest to finish the job as quickly as possible. The workmanship must suffer as a result.

There is also the serious matter of workmen's insurance in these installations. By its nature, this type of work is dangerous. Hence insurance is expensive and difficult to obtain. You must make it your business to see that the men are covered *before* they touch the job. No verbal or written assurance of being covered will do. You *must* see the policy.

The reliability of the company for any needed corrections after installation is your concern too. Often the home-owner cannot find the contractor a year later, and those who can be found still in business are not inclined nor equipped to fix something that goes wrong, like a loose shingle, or leaky roof.

As a result of many unhappy experiences in this area, without implying that all such companies are bad, I finally turned to Sears Roebuck for my sidewalling and roofing jobs. In some cases they supplied the materials and gave every possible assistance, advice and cooperation to my regular carpenter who did the work. In other cases I had Sears contract the whole job from beginning to end. It has been highly satisfactory. Appearance was first-grade. Where a ten-year guarantee went with the job, I have had no difficulty nor delay in getting a leak repaired. They were not hard to find, even years after the job was finished, and they did not stall nor evade.

From a more important safety angle, they were fully insured. I had no worry on this score. In those jobs where my carpenter did the labor, I made sure that he and his helper were covered by my company.

The quality of the work was better too. Even where Sears hired out the jobs to installation crews, those crews were more thoroughly checked for integrity and thoroughness. They took more pains, if for no other reason, because the crew's biggest and steadiest customer was Sears, and they wanted to keep quality up and complaints down, so as not to lose the account. I found no such attitude among the fly-by-nights.

The prices at Sears were, of course, lowest of all, and financing is easy, where you want the tenants to pay for the job.

Aluminum siding is gradually becoming more popular and less expensive. Aluminum has its faults like all others. Generally, it is too expensive for Aunt Tobys.

Where you must paint, such as trim, doors, sash, et cetera, make it your business to inquire into the newer paints (called "acrylic") that resist peeling and scaling. Insist on their being used and do not let the painter switch you. Surfaces should be properly sanded or scraped and, above all, dried out before the application of paint. Generally five or more good drying days must pass after a rain or mist has penetrated, before painting is attempted.

INTERIORS

If you acquire Aunt Tobys, your limit of concern with interior decoration will be the entrance halls. There is little in this area that merits discussion except a few minor points. Ceilings that are cracked or blackened can be very expensive to put in shape. I sampled a product some thirty-one years ago, with strong doubts about the claims of the manufacturers. After years of experience with the washing, scraping, shellacking, coating and recoating of ceilings, I did not believe there was anything that would not yellow, much less that anything could be applied over old whitewash, calcimine, or paint, without thorough and expensive laborious preparation. "Just wipe (not wash) the surface, mix the stuff *as per directions,* and spread it on," said the seller. The ceilings we did in 1929, 1930, et cetera, are still snow white and no trace of yellowing or peeling is evident! I have since recommended the product to thousands. I do not have any personal or business connection with the makers. My only concern is to save you money and bother and to make your building more attractive.

You will have to avoid only two errors. When you buy it, insist on Evan-lite Ceilcote* and *no other*. Shun any product that the hardware man says is the "same thing with a different label, that's all," or "It's the same formula—they're all alike." If you cannot obtain it locally ask your supplier to stock it. He won't sell as much "repeater" ceiling paint, but he sure will make some delighted customers. Substitution, often innocent, has been a constant curse in this matter.

The other error to guard against is the seemingly universal reluctance of painters to read and follow the directions for mixing. They are too accustomed to going by guess, and stirring in "a little more, I guess." Insist on precise adherence to the printed clear directions, even when your painter protests that "you can't spread it on when it's like that—it's impossible!" Tell him to go ahead and dip his brush and *he* will be surprised.

A little side hint. When he must fill a crack or small hole in the ceiling, ask him *not* to mix the plaster or spackle compound with water. Use the same paint as a mixing fluid. It will hold better and will "take" the paint better with better concealment of the spot.

The same paint may be tinted and used for hall walls, but many owners prefer to use the new water-paints which can be rolled on quickly and touched up easily and neatly. Others ask around and locate a dealer who specializes in old stocks of wallpaper. Here you can buy excellent oil cloth wallcoverings at very low rates, and these form fine durable, washable coverings for hall walls. Room wallpapers that normally cost 75¢ to $1 per roll may be bought from these dealers, (particularly if you know how to haggle) for 5¢ or so. Some owners give the paper and paste to the tenants and let them supply the labor. I prefer

---

* Made by T C Dunham Paints, 581 Sawmill River Rd., Yonkers, N.Y. Inquire for your nearest dealer.

to give them some of the new water paint and a roller and tray. This may be used over old wallpaper or paint and almost any amateur can make a room look lovely in a few hours. When you give it to one, however, be ready to give it to all. The other tenants will soon be on your neck for some too.

There is one item in interior decoration that costs almost nothing and gives a decided uplift to any hall or room. It is the replacement of light fixtures. For less than $2 you can buy a very attractive and appropriate fixture, modern and smart. Installation is a matter of minutes and any man able to read simple directions can install them. Of course be sure to shut off the electricity before attempting to install one, and if you do not know how, get some instruction first. I have a little hint in this matter, too. If the light is to be controlled by a pull chain or cord, you will do well to install a style of switch called *Levolier*. Unlike the cheaper pigtail switch, levoliers generally outlast the building. They cost only a few pennies more, and once installed, you are finished with that device for many years.

A FEW MORE HINTS

When a wall switch, normally called a flush toggle switch, is to be replaced, you will find that this is a very simple operation if you are careful to shut off the electricity before touching it. In any case you will want to install the best quality for the few cents it costs and be finished with replacing switches at that point for decades. To this end, insist on "T rated" switches, by whomever they may be made in your area. Your electric supply house will understand this and, as in the case of levolier pull-switches, once installed you can forget about it for the life of the building.

Faucet washers should likewise be attended to in the manner that promises best to make each repair as permanent as possible. If you are at all mechanically inclined, or even if you are just willing to learn simple things that save bother and money, you can easily obtain:

A few No. 22 drills.

A 10/24 tap.

A tapwrench.

A supply of the *best* faucet washers your supplier can obtain. At present writing the only leader is the leather for cold and the fibre for hot water. But there are new synthetics being tested and you may soon find them better.

And, if you want to go the whole way, a reseating tool for faucets.

A box of stainless steel, philister head $\frac{3}{4}$ by $1\frac{0}{24}$ screws.

A roll of graphite packing.

Each time you service *any* faucet or ball cock, you drill out the screw hole, tap a new $1\frac{0}{24}$ thread in it, and install the washer with one of the stainless screws. Soon all your fixtures will be standard in this regard and yearly service much easier and quicker. Your water bills will shrink significantly. Unless you are very unmechanical, there needn't be any plumbing bills for these minor maintenance items.

The reseating tool will save you installing new faucets where the seeping water has made runnels and crevices in the seat against which the washer presses. You will learn to use it easily and thereafter it is almost fun to fix leaky faucets.

One final bit of advice in the general matter of maintenance and repairs. Go and see the trouble. Try to resist the temptation to do the lazy thing. Whatever you ordinarily sell your time for, unless you are a doctor or dentist, you can sell it for more per hour if you investigate needed repairs personally, and check them during and after the work is done.

In the months I toured the world with my family, I would sometimes have an assistant watch over the properties and service complaints. One day, during a torrential downpour, a tenant called to say the water was flooding down from her ceiling. The moment she hung up, my man dialed the roofer. My secretary stopped him, and suggested he go and see the trouble personally. He took his feet down from his desk with some annoyance, grumbling, "Wha'dya expect *me* to do?" When he went to the building he found that an attic window was wide open—that's all. The roofer's bill would have been substantial.

21

STRAIGHTENING OUT TENANCIES

In the ownership of rental units, your entire income must come from tenants. You can avoid many of the mistakes that I made if you resolve to resist temptation. The resulting long-run profits will be considerably increased by instituting and maintaining the right rules, and attitudes between you and the tenants. The amount you clear each year can be doubled or halved, depending on your methods. Further, your enjoyment of peaceful, pleasant ownership can be established or precluded depending on how you establish your landlord-tenant relationship.

The technique of putting the tenant-landlord relations on a good working basis is really simple if you are prepared for a few things that usually happen at this time.

Invariably the tenants talk to one another about their feelings and futures under the new ownership. Their attitude toward you at this time will be governed by the possibility of rent raises. They generally expect the rent to be raised. Often they will ask you outright what you plan in this regard.

If there is a brassy tenant among them, he will usually boast to the others that *he* is going to make *you* toe the mark. He has listed a string of repairs that he will demand. Far from fearing a rent raise, he has it all planned how much *more* he is going to get for his present rent. In your relations with the other tenants the first principle is *to stay away from them as much as possi-*

139

ble. But you will avoid the brassy one even more. Perhaps he has poisoned the others. But you will bear in mind that this can be a pleasant and profitable relationship *only if you start out right* and thereafter keep things in line.

Above all, never fear a vacancy. If a tenant tells you he is moving out, simply request the proper notice in writing, giving you the legal period in which to find a new tenant. In most states, under a tenancy at will, where tenants rent by the month and pay each month's rent in advance on the first day of the month, the law requires that the tenant notify you in writing on or before the first of any month that he will vacate on the last day of that month. We will establish written lease arrangements soon in the building but usually find the present tenants occupying as tenants-at-will. So when Mr. Brassy phones you to say, "I'm moving out," you reply quietly that you want him to send you written notice—any letter will do. Mention that you will arrange for a new tenant to move in. He may be waiting for you to ask him why. Don't. If he lists all the things that "he has been suffering with" as he paid this high rent, you should agree. Tell him he is right. The apartment is worthless, and he is doing the right thing in vacating.

Your handling of Mr. Brassy will have a salutary effect on your future relations with him, (if he does not vacate, and usually he won't) and, more important, with the other tenants, whether or not he moves out.

You *must* get things off on the right foot!

Some years ago, I rented a small store to one Leon as a corner variety-grocery. I mentioned to him that I'd like his phone number when he got one installed, and trusted he would establish a pleasant and lasting relationship with the local neighbors. He replied that he was NOT putting in a phone. Also, he warned me that soon I would hear a rumor that he is a mean and difficult neighbor. Intrigued, I asked him for an explanation. His answer taught me a lot, because similar to my relations with tenants with whom I must deal repeatedly for years, he sold to the same neighbors week in week out. He had learned by his mistakes in other locations to start off on the right foot. He now knew that he must establish mutually work-able and liveable relations, or none.

"First, I'm not putting in a phone because I've learned, the hard way, that this invites people to phone me to 'run over with a loaf of bread—it's an emergency—won't take you a minute.' After a housewife has bought from me for a while she will send little Junior over. 'Mama says give me a pound of ham and a quart of milk and she will be in tomorrow and pay you,' and I will gently but firmly refuse, with apologies. The woman will be furious. She will tell her neighbors, 'I spend thirty dollars a week in Leon's store and he wouldn't trust me for two dollars. I'm never going to shop there again!" She will avoid me for a few weeks but she will surely come back—this time with the money in hand or not at all. When I went broke at my last store, I had a fat book of accounts 'receivable' and if I had been able to collect ⅓ of it, I would have prospered. I'm going to start out on the right basis and KEEP it on that basis."

So whenever a tenant says he is moving, we reply, "Very well, please write me the notice and I will arrange for a new tenant to move in."

Above all, never placate nor make peace offerings or induce-ments. You may rely on it, such a practice is profitless and end-less. An experience my mother had, although a little extreme, was typical of what happens when an owner fears a vacancy and, as a result, establishes a wrong relationship.

We owned an Aunt Toby and lived in the middle floor. One day a Mrs. H. moved in to the top flat. She paid her first month's rent, $38.00, when she moved in, and one month later she knocked on our door, handed mother the rent and notified us she was vacating at the end of the month. Mother inquired why. Mrs. H. explained that there being no French doors be-tween the living room and dining room, she could not keep house as she wished and had heard of another flat where she would be happy. Mother asked if she would be satisfied if the doors were installed. Yes. Mother promised to have them in-stalled for her and she left, withdrawing the notice. I protested vehemently, but was told that the $100 or so it would cost to put the doors in was a lighter loss than having the flat redone and perhaps losing several months' rent during the vacancy. She made the common mistake of thinking that another tenant would probably want the same thing anyway, and it was best to install it since we would be forced to do so eventually. Then she threw in that argument that we should *shun like the plague*. "It improves the property, you'll have a better building for it." Of course, the next month Mrs. H. gave notice again. No dish cabinets in the kitchen, this time. Cost, $80. Then another radiator, and so on for five months.

At the end of six months, Mrs. H. vacated anyway. Incidentally, she claimed she had tripped on a step and sued for damages, settling with our insurance company for a sum far greater than she had paid in rent during her stay.

You won't find many Mr. Brassys but if you should be so unlucky, you can benefit in your relations with the other tenants through your firmness with him. To submit would be to set an example that would require you to evict all tenants and start over again if the building is to show its proper return.

Immediately after taking title, you should send a short letter to each tenant, informing him formally that you are the new owner and, in effect, 'giving him his orders.' Here is a good example of the type of letter to use.

Dear Mr. (Tenant):

You are hereby advised that I have purchased the building at 38 Elm St. Will you kindly fill out the enclosed form for my records and return it to me within three days? In due course, you will receive our standard lease for your signature.

Rent for your apartment should be mailed so as to reach this office on or before the first of each month, and addressed to:
. . . .

Yours very truly,
John New-Owner

Sometimes I enclose a few self-addressed envelopes to start the tenant off right, with the suggestion that she should obtain some more and address them accordingly. We enclose an application that we regularly use for new tenants, so that we may have a clear record of who the tenant is, where he works, and other pertinent information. In a few days, we send him two copies of the lease, for him to sign (both) and return for our signature. This process will be thoroughly covered in a later chapter showing how to get all tenancies on a firm lease basis. We are here concerned more with those methods peculiar to the new owner taking over.

In the matter of the *time* of rent payment, you have a good opportunity to implant the right attitude about your ownership. If you receive the rent as much as one day late, a short note should be sent, thus:

Dear Mr. Tenant:

Your rent did not reach this office on the first day of the month as required by law. Since I have precise obligations at the bank that must be paid on the exact due date, it is necessary that the rents reach me on time, so that I do not default.

Kindly see to it that the rent is mailed so as to *reach* me not later than the first of each month in the future so that I will not be required to write you again in this matter.

                                        Yours very truly,

It is not uncommon for even non-brassy tenants to jump on a new owner with a long list of complaints. These are answered in the same manner as shown for Mr. Brassy. We agree that the place is worthless and urge, "You're quite right, Mr. Tenant. Best thing for you would be to move out, and we'll get someone in who likes the flat just as it is. No, I do not intend to improve it any. When you send me the written notice, I will make arrangements for a new tenant." Do not get into the natural hassle about "Why have you lived there for fifteen years with your old landlord and not insisted on these things?" You won't get anywhere with this. Just suggest he move out. One thing I can unequivocally promise you. If he moves, he was going to move anyway. And you can and will re-rent if he moves out, to a tenant that is not demanding. But to give in is to guarantee that you will lose out on this matter, whichever way it turns out. whether he moves or stays.

Your position is firm. The right relationship—or none.

There will sometimes be a few repairs that are in the category of things you fairly should attend to. They are generally:

Defective plumbing (we will have more on plugged drains later).
Electric fixtures that do not work.
Leaky roof.
Inadequate heat (where furnished).
Any other similar breakdown that is not just an aesthetic matter but more a structural defect of the building.

When you get notified, as a new owner, of any of the above, you will NOT promise to correct the condition—only to check into it. If you get the hurry-up pressure from the tenant, do not let HIS excitement stir *you*. We do not jump at command. We will look into it when we get ready. Nothing in his urgency must be permitted to make *us* get excited. Usually the repair has been needed for months before you took over anyway. I have had a tenant excitedly call me and shout that the water is gushing and flooding the place. When I hurried over, expecting to see the furniture floating about, the faucet was dribbling.

Perhaps you may get the impression from the above that the ownership and tenant dealings are fraught with haggling and unpleasant argument. I have set out only the incidents out of my experience that best seem to exemplify the points I wish to make. It should be remembered that a dozen or so glaringly bad experiences are not significant in the whole picture. I owned up to 146 units at one time over a period of thirty-one years. I have picked out some incidents from these and from the thousands of tenant-contacts that my students and friends have had. On the whole, you will have years and years of the most cordial dealings with tenants, particularly in Aunt Tobys and similar units. It seems best to point out the horrible examples, so that you will keep the errors of your dealings to a minimum, but they are very rare considering the 145 good tenants versus the troublesome one. And I soon got rid of him. Generally, I had not rented the flat to Mr. Brassy originally. I acquired him with the building when I bought. Perhaps his attitude was one of the reasons the seller sold to me, so I am sometimes indebted to the bad tenant for making it possible for me to buy. I will soon either straighten him out or kick him out.

The wisdom of old Mrs. McGee, learned by intuition and experience, should be our guide in tenant relationships, particularly where we are on an at-will basis. Remember it well. All that she learned is embodied in the five words.

"They stay to suit themselves. And if they don't be suited, they goes."

She made a street cleaner's $30 per week into a million dollars with that rule. It's good enough for me.

THE TEN COMMANDMENTS
OF BUILDING OWNERSHIP

There are just a few general and specific bits of advice about holding which can be incorporated in ten simple rules. These are offered with the realization that temperaments vary. Some owners "improve" the buildings without end, and thus improve themselves into pennilessness. Some owners just "can't stand" the appearance of that back hall. This is not the routine "New-Owneritis." It is a permanent condition. These owners should never have gone into this business.

Then there are those who fail to discount the exaggerations of tenants. In this regard we must accept the fact that we as landlords, automatically induce a state of mind (and sometimes of dishonesty) that banks and insurance companies accept as normal. The bank is quite accustomed to the fact that when it sends out a statement to a depositor erroneously showing his balance to be much larger than it really is, the depositor rarely phones to call attention to the error.

Insurance companies are equally, if not more, accustomed to the same attitude among claimants. Typically, an insurance adjuster, who handles the claims of a cleaning and dyeing chain, said, "It's remarkable, if not amazing. Folks who have been coming into the store with $50 suits and hold menial jobs at $75 or $100 per week will file a claim for a lost overcoat. Almost without exception the overcoat cost $400 and was 'only worn twice.' We've never yet had a claim for an overcoat under $300. And most of them from slum areas. Nor are the claims of the middle class any different."

The nearest thing to an analysis of this is that people seem to lay aside their normal scruples and morals when dealing with banks and insurance companies. It is much the same metamorphosis that takes place when a normally courteous considerate person walks through a department store, opens the door for a lady who happens to be passing out at the same moment, and behaves courteously to all about him. No sooner does he get behind the wheel of his car than he turns into a snarling beast. The selfsame woman for whom he opened the door may be occupying the car next in line. Now he blasts his horn at her, forces her to stall, et cetera.

To some extent the same lack of simple courtesy, and sometimes honesty, obtains in the claims of tenants to their landlords. If you are a person who tries to confine your statements to the simple truth, you are probably one who assumes this to be true in others. This can cause extensive loss and aggravation. You must develop a tolerant attitude. When a tenant complains about lack of heat, it is never "the heat didn't come on this morning. Will you look into it when you can, please?"

It is always a variant of this: "We haven't had a bit of heat in *four* days! I've caught a bad cold, and I think my child is getting pneumonia!" et cetera. You know full well that this tenant would not have endured even one day of lack of heat without calling you. The point is, let the tenant get excited. You stay calm. These ten rules are an effort to gather the most common do's and don'ts into a simple code:

1. Never fear a vacancy. Get rid of the bad ones quickly. To submit to a threat is no solution to anything. To accept a hard luck story instead of rent solves nothing. If he's that kind, you will be called unpleasant things later anyway when your kindness must be cut off.

2. Get a good tenant or none. It is far better to leave the flat vacant another month or two, than compromise your requirements. To take the unsuitable applicant because you dislike

having a vacancy simply exchanges one headache for another.

3. Do *not* make any improvement or installation that is not needed to keep the building in good shape for the class of tenant you will get. Avoid overzealousness to improve, spend, or repair. Second only to the pitfall of no. 1, this is the major cause of owners *not* getting rich.

4. Give good attention to repairs. See the need with your own eyes. Talk to other owners or contractors. Learn the best measures for that type of repair. Except where you have a reliable mechanic, such as a carpenter, or it is a small repair, never give the job out on an hourly or cost-plus basis. The contractor may have to put a flat price on the job that is higher, perhaps, than the hourly basis would cost, but it is better. You must know that the entire job, finished and workmanlike and properly guaranteed by a reliable outfit, will cost a definite amount. Visit the job often while in progress and learn about it. Examine it upon completion, and if possible test it before paying the bill. It is common practice for a roof job to be paid for *after* the next heavy rainstorm.

5. Treat the tenants fairly. Supply the services and repairs to which they are entitled, and to the extent that the letting reasonably calls for. But—

6. Never let the tenant's urgency become yours. Lack of heat, a roof leak, a burst pipe or other "life-and-death" emergencies must not get you excited any more than the phone company gets excited when you report your phone out of order. Nor for that matter does the hospital get excited when a call comes in that someone is dying.

If there is a burst pipe, you will call the water department at once, asking for emergency shut-off. If there's smoke you will call the fire department. But you will invariably take the proper steps without hurry or panic. If a refrigerator does not work, you must not be stampeded by the threat that all the tenant's food will spoil. If the tenant had her way you would have a new $500 refrigerator delivered in ten minutes. But that is not your obligation. If you furnish a mechanical thing for her use, it is to be expected that there will be breakdowns. She must expect them. You will make the repair or service in due course —unhurried.

7. Never get involved in inter-tenant feuds. It is best to refuse to listen.

8. Never try to improve the standard of living of anybody.

9. Keep away from the buildings except for minimum inspections. You will be buttonholed if seen about the premises, and there never *was* an apartment of *any* class where a tenant couldn't find something he wants you to correct.

Train the tenants to send the rent to you, preferably by mail, even if you must supply stamped envelopes. You can easily obtain a permit for the self-addressed type which you can give them generously and thus pay only a few pennies more than regular postage on those you receive.

10. Never sue anybody. You will avoid practically all need for it by following the practices learned here. At most you may want to file a small-claims action for rent occasionally, as a measure to teach a skipping deadbeat a lesson, and show the others in the town that you will not permit abuses, but that is about all. You do not need to employ a lawyer for the small-claims action. Talk to the clerk of your local court and he will guide you in bringing your suit. If you checked the tenant before accepting him, you will usually receive the money before the date for court appearance. If not, and he contacts you with a *cash* offer of settlement before the trial, you should take it if it is at all within reason. You have better things to do with your time than chase him for $1 a week.

And here's an 11th commandment that I learned from the same Mrs. McGee who gave us the rule in the first chapter. When a tenant is slow in paying the rent and offers promises instead of money, remember what she said. It needs no explanation. "If they can't pay one month, they can't pay two."

22

NEW TENANTS

Your MIF will be considerably enhanced or depleted, depending on your methods of processing new tenants. There are three major effects that result from your methods in this area.

First, your freedom from bother and smoothness of operation. Almost every time you have a petulant tenant, you can trace it to an error in your routine when you accepted him as tenant. Of course, where you inherited him with the building this is not the case, but every effort should be made to straighten him out as detailed in the previous chapter.

If you have unheated Aunt Tobys, it will be the common thing, not the exception, to have tenants who do not speak to you more than once every two or three years. Yes, that is literally true, providing you have made the right start. You receive the rent regularly and reliably on time each month. The lease renews itself automatically without any message or contact. It is the nearest thing to getting an annuity that I have ever encountered. In almost every new tenancy you can establish this delightful situation if you follow a few simple rules. Again it seems necessary for me to exemplify many points by horrible examples, so please do not permit them to scare you into thinking that any material percentage are bad. These stand out in my experience for the very reason that they were rare.

When you learn that you are going to have a vacancy, you

will advertise and show the flat. If a party sees the flat and wants to apply for it, you will sit down with him for the *vital interview*. These five minutes are the key to whether you are going to get along without friction. It will be thoroughly discussed when we set out the steps you take with new tenants. It is mentioned here because of its particular relevancy to a smooth relationship.

One day a Mr. R. answered an ad for an apartment in the Uni group. The flat had been occupied previously by one tenant for 34 years. It had never been redecorated in that time. When this tenant died, I decided to clean it up and spent some $300. After Mr. and Mrs. R. had looked it over, they came to my office and sat down to talk. Mr. R. was definite. He felt it was a good flat in a fine location, and he urged Mrs. R. to agree. She wavered. Did Mr. R. think the refrigerator would do? It seemed very old. And the gas range. Was that going to be usable? She baked so much. The low windows, would the kids be likely to fall out?

Mr. R. assured her it would be OK and they filed an application and deposited the first month's rent. When I sent in for the credit report, I hoped it would come back unsatisfactory and thus take a decision out of my hands. Darn it, he proved to have a fine background. Being an accountant, he had paid all bills promptly, worked steadily and had lived in his present quarters for ten years. But I had perceived what you have spotted in the interview and called him and asked him to accept the return of the deposit and withdraw his application, with no reflection on his credit or desirability as a tenant. He urged me not to reject him. I told him then that I felt that although he was satisfied with the flat, Mrs. R. was not. I hazarded the guess that she wanted him to buy her a new single house. "Yes," he conceded, "I'll admit we've looked at them. But I know my income and limitations and want to pay my bills and keep my head above water. We simply cannot afford a single. I hope you will give us this flat."

I saw the little red flag that we all see waving in our mind's eye, when we do something against our experience and better

judgment. Moved by his sincere assurances, which I still feel
he meant, I agreed to lease the flat to him. I explained that he
would be taking over a freshly decorated apartment. It did not
make sense to spread the cost of decoration over one year.
Three years was minimal. He agreed. Then I spoke firmly and
told him that if he took the flat he would be required to live up
to the lease, and he still agreed.

As you have doubtless guessed, he no sooner moved in than
Mrs. R. descended on me for a new refrigerator, badgering me
incessantly until I gave her one. Then (a la Mrs. H. of the previous chapter) she got to work on the gas range. Months later
I agreed to swap it for one I knew was good, and no sooner did
I assent to this, when, *in the same conversation,* she started on
the sink. Then I knew where we were going (or not going) in
this matter and I clamped down.

A few months later, Mr. R. phoned me. Sheepishly he
hemmed and hawed. "Guess you know why I'm calling." I did.
"Guess you can easily find a new tenant anyway." I coldly replied that he was going to pay the rent for the three years. If
there was to be any new tenant in that flat before his lease
expired, *he* would have to find him and *I* would have to approve of him first. I had erred in ignoring the things that the
vital interview had shown me.

The second benefit you will receive from using and being
guided by the rental technique you will learn here will be the
lowering of your losses through bad debts. I had to learn most
of these things the hard way, by making the mistakes. But by
1935 or so, I had been an owner for six years and had perfected
rules that governed later lettings and reduced my losses through
non-payment of rent to less than one tenth the average that
prevailed in this industry at the time. There is practically no
need to lose money through bad debts in this business if you
follow the rules.

By getting some credit information and withholding acceptance of the applicant as tenant until you have received a satisfactory credit report, you will, as far as it is possible, avoid
those tenants who will give you non-payment trouble. It is

rarely that I have seen a case where the credit check said OK and later experience was at variance. If a man has so governed his spending that the record shows him a prompt payer of auto installments, appliance payments, et cetera, as well as his rent in the past, you can well rely on getting his rent promptly too. Neither the depression, illness, being out of work, nor for that matter the size of his income seems to affect this rule. A prompt payer is just that, with very rare exceptions. Many who have little income have learned a stewardship of money that is highly commendable, and their bills are always paid promptly. Perhaps this is because they are in the habit of undertaking obligations only when they are sure they can meet them, and they forego extravagances providently rather than buy them optimistically.

Conversely, many, with what we would classify as large incomes, are constantly a jump ahead of the sheriff.

The third area in which you will enhance your profit by use of tested renting methods, is by cutting vacancy periods to a negligible minimum. After all, your expense and costs continue unbrokenly whether the flat is vacant or productive. With good practices your tenants will rarely stay less than five or ten years. *Your* idle periods between tenants will usually be *nil*.

There is no reason why you cannot match or better the percentage to which I reduced losses by vacancy and bad debts, even in the depression. The further you get from a basic Aunt Toby, the greater the tendency toward turnover in tenants, with consequent incidental small losses. My overall percentage of loss for both vacancy and bad debts between 1936 and 1955 was less than 3% in the heated buildings and less than 1% in the unheated Aunt Tobys!

STEPS IN PROCESSING NEW TENANTS

Since the effect on your MIF, your enjoyment of your investment, and other benefits will be largely governed by your handling of new tenants, the steps will be set out in detail. The process is practically the same for every type of vacancy, be it

store, office or apartment. As owners, we want to get along happily with tenants who are satisfied, and make a profit.

*Step 1: We learn of an impending vacancy and we advertise
it.* If it is vacant, we leave it open and send prospects to see it
at their leisure. If you have time to waste, you may accompany
them, for a purpose. You will listen to their comments and
learn as much or more than you would learn in the Vital Interview.

Step 2: When the tenant indicates he wishes to apply for the
apartment and you have the approval of both husband and
wife, ask him if he is prepared to deposit one month's rent with
his application. Be very alert at this point. What he answers,
and how he answers, will be the key to much that happens
later.

If he hesitates, and seems reluctant, saying something like,
"Er, well, is it really necessary? We've always paid a $10 de-
posit," or if he has a whispered or private chat with his wife at
this point, you may depend on it that either he hasn't got the
money or he hasn't quite made up his mind and simply wants
to hold this one until he makes his choice between your apartment and another.

Those who readily pay the month's rent are ready for the
next step in your process, but the ones who cannot or won't,
deserve careful discussion here. First let us dispose of the tenant who wants you to "hold it until tomorrow and we'll let you
know." The polite, but firm, answer is, "Sorry, but that is
against our policy. We cannot tell another party who definitely
wants the apartment that we cannot give it to him because
another party *might* want it. When you have decided definitely that you want it, come back and if it is available, we will
make the arrangements."

Then there is the chap who wants you to take a small deposit
of $5 or $10. Again, "Sorry, our policy requires one full month's
rent with the application." In this one you must remain un-
shakeable.

Before I learned never to break this rule, I had a vacant flat
and a Mrs. N. came to see me. She was very well-dressed and

well spoken and assured me that everything was OK. She gave me $5 as a deposit, got a receipt, and promised to pay the balance of the first month's rent on the first of the month and move in. From then on I refused all applicants. The first of the month came and went but no Mrs. N. I tried to phone her several times without success and finally went to the apartment house where she lived.

She was out but I talked with the janitor. "Mrs. N. moving out?" he said, puzzled. I explained about her making a deposit. "Oh, I see," he replied, "she was *threatening* to move from here and wanted her living room done over. She got your receipt so that she could show it to the owner here and convince him she was actually moving, so he agreed to do the room. Now she's staying." By the way, Mrs. N. demanded the return of the $5. I sued her and collected two months' rent, and court costs. But it was I who had erred in accepting a small deposit.

The lasting benefits of the rule of one month's rent with application will be enjoyed by you in many ways.

You brush off all those who would tie you up and cause you to refuse good tenants to hold on to a bad one, as in the case of Mrs. N. The rule serves to stop your dealings with those who are wavering between your place and another. It is not unusual for an applicant who has made a small deposit on one flat to peruse the ads thereafter to see what he missed. Sometimes he sees an ad offering an apartment that is "just what he wanted" and he goes to see it. That's when you begin to have bother that could well have been avoided.

Then there is the prospective tenant who is always in financial difficulty. This condition seems to be unaffected by the size of the income. It is caused by the lack of stewardship of money which usually accompanies over-optimism. This unrealistic fellow will be a headache as a tenant, particularly if there is illness or other unexpected financial drain.

Almost without exception when you encounter a reluctance to deposit the full month's rent with an application, the fellow will never admit he simply hasn't got it. He will argue against the policy that you follow. But when this happens, you have slipped into the Vital Interview stage and the matter is settled in your mind, although he doesn't know it. He is not going to be your tenant.

Perhaps the strongest reason for insistence on our rule is the establishment of the answer to this question: "Who is boss?" In this regard, there are two types of people; those who follow the rules and those who protest them. If you own the building you make the rules. If a man wants to rent from you, he's going to abide by your rules or go elsewhere. This is the right time to find out whether *he* is going to tell *you* what to do, or if you are going to decide how the building is run.

I have had many experiences with people who wanted the flat and who seemed friendly and amenable, until they heard this rule. Then they became bitter or difficult, practically ordering me to take the small deposit. They thus showed me, before it was too late, that these were not the people for me. Perhaps the outstanding one was Mr. P. Here I made the mistake of renting the apartment to him without seeing him. His wife made all the negotiations, since he was about to be discharged from service. I never learned whether he was a sergeant in the army, but he certainly was the traditional one with his landlord. I finally got rid of him and he moved into Mr. McG's building. More about this later.

Step 3: The Vital Interview. You will invariably find the applicant ready to chat a few minutes if he has passed the early test of willingness to deposit the full month's rent. Ask him about his present apartment and landord. If he mentions that his present landlord is a mean impossible miser, you may depend on it that you are next to bear this title. Note carefully his reason for moving. If it's because the other tenant is unfit to live with, his neighbor in the new building will soon be no better. Talk about the apartment he is taking. Ask whether he will be able to fit his family and furniture comfortably into it. If he broaches a list of the things he will expect you to do, you have seen the red flag.

Somewhat apologetically, I usually answer this with, "I guess you are right. The place does need all those things, but unfortunately my policy is to go along as is. You should find a place where they keep things up. Frankly my policy is to give you the keys to the door and almost nothing else. We will repair plumbing leaks (but not stoppages) or roof leaks. But that's about all. Beyond that, you're on your own."

Occasionally you will chat with a prospective tenant who makes a point of the fact that in taking this flat he is coming down in the world, since he is used to better accommodations. You will do well to pass this one up too. Likewise the one who moves every six months.

You will have no difficulty in most interviews, seeing that this person is agreeable, willing to follow your rules, and definitely wants your flat in the condition you are offering it. He is ready for Step 4.

Step 4: Hand him the credit form to fill out. Here is the form I have used successfully, but your credit reporting company may suggest certain locally desirable additional information that you should obtain for them in order for them to give you a full report.

APPLICATION FOR APARTMENT

Name .... Phone: Days........ Eves.........

Address ....

Employed by ...., Phone ....,

Position .... How long? ....

Present landlord ....,

His address .... Phone ....

How long at present residence? .... Rent $........

Business references ....

....

....

....

....

Banking account with .... Checking ....

.... Savings ....

Does applicant own real estate? .... Where? ....

Premises applied for .... To occupy .... 19....

Number to occupy ...... adults ...... children ...... Pets? .....

Ages of children ....

Rent per month ....

Do you have a car? .... Do you require parking? ....

Order these forms direct from:
(c) REALFORMS Box 1, Brookline, Mass. 02146 Form #AFA

Give him a copy of the lease he will be expected to sign, to take home and study at his leisure. While he peruses it, make out a very special receipt for his deposit. This is the form.

Receipt for deposit with application for APARTMENT
Date .... 19 .... Received from ....,
$.............. deposit with application for apartment pending investigation. No tenancy is hereby created. Applicant will be notified upon completion of investigation. No parking included. No dogs allowed.

....
(Owner) (Agent)

Receipt for deposit with application for STORE (OFFICE) (IND'L. SPACE)

Date .... 19 .... Received from ....,
$.............. deposit with application for store (office) (industrial space) pending investigation. No tenancy is hereby created. Applicant will be notified upon completion of investigation. No parking included.

....
(Owner) (Agent)

Order these forms direct from:
(c) REALFORMS Box 1, Brookline, Mass. 02146 Form #DR

When he leaves, you are ready to check his credit background.

In my efforts to set up the most trouble-free type of tenancy, I have learned by experience that the standard family unit is far more trouble-free and self-reliant than the others. I have long established a policy of rejecting the widow, divorcee, or "separated" people. For one thing these women have no man around the house to make minor home repairs. Hence they will bother the landlord for such things as a balky window shade, or a door that sticks. For another, they are much more restless and inclined to move more frequently. Often this is because they have started a feud with a neighbor, or hope to find happier contacts elsewhere. Most of all, I fear, they lack attention. Then they seem to want to keep dogs, which we shall discuss shortly. Finally the need to heckle somebody seems to be standard equipment, and too often the absence of a man around the house makes them turn to the landlord. So I turn them down, explaining that my experience has shown that they are best off taking an apartment in a janitor-serviced building. I remain firm even though they insist they are self-reliant and promise to look after themselves. When human nature is in conflict with spoken promises, one knows which must emerge on top.

In the yellow pages of your local phone book there are listed under Credit Reports, companies who will investigate prospective tenants for you at $3 to $10 per report. You simply phone one and tell him you are a landlord and want a tenant's report on the subject. He will take the information on the phone and within a few days give you a phoned or written report. These reports have always been a clear indication to me of yes or no. Those who have lived lengthy periods in one place, paid their bills to installment sellers or department stores, will usually pay my rent promptly, too. Assuming there is no negative item, such as impending divorce, more drinking than you consider moderate, "had loud jam sessions" or "hi-fi player," these are clear yeses. We phone these and give them an incentive, by the wording of our acceptance, to show *us* how good a risk they are. "Good morning Mr. (Tenant). This is Mr. (Owner). I just got a credit report on you. Fine record! Be glad to have you. Drop in and sign the lease."

The doubtful ones, and they will be few, are classified with the definite no's. They are rejected thus: A short letter, with check enclosed, regretting the application was not accepted. That's all.

Step 5. Sign up the lease. This lease is the result of much more than legal experience with leases, both in drawing them and in fighting them in court. It was written to promote good relations, not lawsuits. We do not want to win lawsuits. We do not even want to sue anyone. Our objective is simple: a happy trouble-free profitable landlord-and-tenant relationship.

For one thing, experience has shown that suing a tenant, as in many other lawsuits, is profitless *and* bad public relations.

In effect, the lease forms a simple list of rules, such as you would see on the door of a hotel room. In its printed form, the tenant sees that the rules are standard for all tenants for the benefit of all and he is much more likely to obey them cheerfully as a result.

More important, the printed rules incorporated in the lease will cut down your losses and vacancy periods. They will even save you a little on advertising and repairs. As much as it is possible to do, the rules will insure the trouble-free business-like relationship that we seek.

Note that the form is in clear non-legalistic language. I have seen court cases wherein the judge scanned a finely printed lengthy verbose document and declared, "I wouldn't force a tenant to live up to all this stuff. I don't believe the average layman would understand it, even though it may be legal and technically binding."

Thus it is from the most practical viewpoint that I have gradually evolved a lease form which tries to establish standard rules, is clear and easy to understand and follow, treats the parties fairly, and cuts down losses. I have paid little if any attention to making it legally binding, for the simple reason that as a practical matter, the only negative objective I seek is the right to evict a tenant who is not living up to the rules. There is some further deterrent against vacating at odd times of the year, when it is difficult to rent, but this is only a hoped-for result.

When you fill out this lease, which it still is, you will find it a one-minute job. The form will serve as a good record of your deal with the tenant, showing date of taking occupancy, etc. Note that the entire contract of letting is contained in the first paragraph. The rules follow. Here is the form. The parts you fill in are in italics.

LEASE AND AGREEMENT

Date .... *March 16, 1960* .... 19....

The undersigned Landlord hereby leases to the undersigned Tenant

the PREMISES: .... *Apartment 3* .... at # .... *38 Oak* .... St.,

.... *Brookline, Mass.,* .... FOR ...... *17* ...... MONTHS beginning

.... *April 1,* .... 19.. *60* ... at $ ... *$150.00* ... per month. This lease shall automatically renew and continue thereafter from year to year until either party shall give written notice on or before the

first day of .... *July* .... (mo.) in any year, terminating this

lease as of the last day of .... *the following August.* ....

Others to occupy .... *Mrs. Tenant and 2 minor children.* ....

The parties hereby covenant and agree:

No PART of the premises shall be sublet, nor underlet.

No ARTICLE OR SUBSTANCE shall be kept on the premises, nor any occupation conducted which is illegal, noisy, or dangerous or which might increase the insurance premiums of the building.

ALL RUBBISH IS TO BE properly separated by the tenant and placed in the proper receptacles. No paper, cans, nor bottles to be placed in garbage containers.

No DOGS, CATS, or other pets to be kept on the premises.

ALL DRAINS, AND WASTE PIPES ON plumbing are accepted as clear by the tenant and any partial or complete stoppage occurring during the tenancy shall be repaired by the tenant.

No RADIO, TELEVISION, OR PHONOGRAPH is to be played after 11 P.M.

No Baby Carriages, Toys, or other articles are to be left in halls.

No Locks are to be installed nor changed. The landlord is to have a key and may, without liability, enter at any reasonable times and inspect, repair, show the apartment, or post To-let signs.

No Parking on the premises without written permission.

Heat and/or Hot Water to be supplied by the landlord only in those premises where he regularly supplies them, but he shall not be responsible for damage resulting from any interruption of same.

Leaks in Pipes, unless caused by negligence of tenant, are to be repaired by the landlord, within a reasonable time after notice, but the landlord shall not be liable nor responsible for any damages resulting from any such leaks or overflows.

The Landlord shall not be under any obligation to make repairs or decoration in the premises, and shall not be responsible for any damages suffered by the tenant, or those claiming under him by his failure to make such repairs.

The Waiver of any term of this contract at any time shall not be deemed a waiver on any other occasion nor of any other term.

Notices from either party shall be deemed properly delivered if mailed by ordinary mail to the premises or address of the landlord.

Should the Rent Become Overdue, and the landlord sue for same, or sue for possession for non-payment of rent, the tenant shall pay all Court costs and all attorney's fees.

Landlord:....... *(signed) John Owner* .....

Tenant: *(signed) Bill Tenant*

Copyright 1955.
Order these forms direct from:
REALFORMS Box 1, Brookline, Mass. 02146 Form #LA

The benefits to your operation from the first paragraph are many. First, you should always lease the apartment for a number of months which will end on August 31. You may choose the coming August 31, or fill in the number of months that make the first period of renting end a year (or two) from the coming August 31. (In Florida and similar areas, this would be January 31).

This one measure will substantially cut vacancy losses. You

have thus obligated each tenant to vacate, if at all, by giving you *two* months' notice on July 1 that he will be out on August 31. All your tenants, irrespective of when they move in, are signed to this obligation. The right to give such notice does not exist while the original rental period runs. Note that the automatic renewal clause says that such a notice may be given only *after* the original period expires. The net result is that any and all tenants who intend to vacate will give you their notices at one time of the year, on July 1. You now have two months in which to find new tenants for these, and get them set for another year. You will be advertising and showing apartments, but only during one period in the year. One advertising expenditure does for several vacancies. Besides, you are able to show one prospect several choices, sizes and locations to choose from. There will be only the one short period each year when you will be bothered with this, and then you can forget about it for another year. You can head south for the winter, secure in the feeling that the income is flowing in steadily and reliably. You get the full enjoyment of this as you talk to others, who are not as fortunate.

One January, as I turned over to brown the other side awhile under the Florida sun, my companion, Dr. Bob Goldfarb, eminent dermatologist, occupied the next lounge. We discussed staying another week. After the usual references to the likelihood that the gin rummy games would probably pay for it, he remarked, seriously, "You know, Bob, your income goes on and on as you loaf here. Your secretary deposited some $9,000 in rents in your account yesterday. As for me, the moment I leave the office, my income stops cold. Wish I had some real estate."

Choosing August 31 as a standard termination date on all leases will (except in the special areas where January 31 or other dates are obviously to be used) be to your benefit in other ways too. Our type of tenant often has school age children. The undesirability of breaking up a child's school year by moving during the winter sends these tenants, if they are planning to move at all, searching during July. They want to be all moved in and settled before the school year starts. This coincides with being settled before winter too. Your choice of tenant, and likelihood of finding true Aunt Toby-ites, is far better at this time of year. A portion of these folks have gone to a summer place and now seek a permanent place to settle in before school starts. You will find the difference in desirability between midwinter prospects and those in July, striking. If you are unfortunate enough to be filling a vacancy in an off-season for your area, it will become apparent why we emphasize arranging the timing of lease termination.

The provision requiring two months' notice is also for the purpose of cutting down vacancy periods. It must be borne in mind that most of our prospective tenants are living in a flat where they must give the present landlord notice *on or before the first* day of any month, that they are vacating at the end of that month. It follows that the type of fairdealing, conforming tenant you want will abide by this. If you have been notified on July 1 that the flat will be vacant August 31, you now have all of the month of July in which to locate a new tenant.

When your prospective tenant sees the flat, and decides on taking it, neither he nor you want to take a loss of one month's rent. If, for instance, he had to take occupancy and pay rent from August 1, he would say, "I can't do that. I have to give my present landlord notice *on August first* that I will be out August 31. And I don't want to be paying rent in two places for the same month." Hence when you show and sign up in July, the tenant can give his old landlord notice on (or before) August 1 and be square with everyone.

The proper disposal of rubbish is our concern and I have found that the rule helps. The tenant must conform to health rules and must respect the requirements of the city disposal services. Besides, in those cases where you have a janitor, an inconsiderate tenant may make it difficult for you to keep the janitor. Even more important, the careless handling of rubbish often forces the janitor to handle cans, broken glass, et cetera, and cut himself. Then we have the problem of absenteeism and increased compensation insurance cost.

Experience has shown that where you permit a tenant to

have a dog, you spark feuds among the tenants. These invariably come to roost on your doorstep. You will not like being phoned at midnight, by an irate tenant who protests that "that — dog has been barking and howling constantly since 8:30 and I demand that you do something about it!" It is not necessary to list the other problems you will encounter in the building where you allow dogs. It is amusing to remember the hundreds of tenants who applied for apartments in my buildings during the war years, when the shortage was so acute that many tenants offered illegal large bonuses to unscrupulous owners to get one. Every applicant who wanted an apartment from me and who had a cherished pup refused the apartment rather than give up Fido. And of the many who protested the point, every one had a dog which neither barked nor "went."

Much bother, argument, and expense has been saved by the insertion of the drainpipe clause. It is the best practice to give the tenants the drains in clear, full working order. Thereafter, it must be the tenant's responsibility to use them properly. If the previous tenant left a plugged or sluggish drain, we must get it cleared and turn the responsibility over to the tenant from that point on. We cannot check on the tenant who empties improper waste down the sink, such as bacon grease, chicken bones, and the like. But having treated him fairly by giving him the equipment in proper condition, we can and do insist that he keep it that way. This rule carries even to the cases where a child (or adult) has dropped an object such as a comb or toy train into the toilet. Experience has shown that for the landlord to "take care of it just this once" establishes a precedent. I remember particularly a lady who just couldn't help letting the dishcloth slip from her fingers down the kitchen sink drain. After I'd paid the plumber several times to remove it, she had another accident and demanded that I take care of it. I refused and she complained to the health department that the sink was now a health menace. My signed lease showed clearly whose obligation this was. It made the health inspector wash his hands of the matter. But having lost this battle the tenant could not thereafter forgive me and she vacated soon.

As we undertake to analyze the "locks and keys" clause, we have in mind the provisions of the first paragraph in the lease. We have provided that we will receive two months' notice of an intended vacancy. This, however, would be worthless to us if we were not permitted to show the flat in July. Unless you have made a clear (provable, written) agreement otherwise, the common law of landlord and tenancy applies. That is, the tenant is the king in his castle. He has a right to absolute privacy of his home and can keep all, including the landlord, out of it.

When I inherit a bad tenant with a building that I have just taken over, and he gives me notice that he is moving out, this law often costs me a few months' rent or more. The tenant may be irked that I have insisted that he make out a formal application and sign a lease. Or he may have intended to move whenever the rent was raised to a fair level. Or I may have ordered him to move. Either way he is usually not too cordial.

Consequently, when I mention that I will be showing the flat to prospective tenants during the month of notice, he will often say, "No, I don't want anyone going into my apartment until *after* I move out. I pay rent there and I want my rights." And he is in the legal right. Unless I am lucky enough to have another similar apartment to show to prospective tenants (which often saves me the loss), I must wait according to his orders. If he vacates on October 31 or November 1, for instance, I may start showing it during November. Then when I find a taker, *he* must give *his* landlord notice on December 1, and move on January 1. So I lose both the months of November and December in the deal. Worse, the renting season is well over by then and very few desirables move around Christmas. So that the exercise of care in tenant selection may cost me four or five months' rent before the apartment is on a good paying basis again.

It is mainly for that reason that we incorporate the clause in the lease requiring the landlord to have a key at all times and the tenant signs that the landlord may enter, show the apartment, etc.

There are some other loss-saving effects of the key clause. If, for instance, you smell smoke in a building, and want to investigate at once, and find the door locked and the lock changed, this can have very serious consequences. If water is seen dripping into the apartment below, you will want to get in to stop it. Sometimes a tenant leaves a window wide open and a sudden downpour threatens to do serious damage. When gas must be shut off for a repair, it is usually necessary to check each apartment before it may be turned on again. It should not be difficult to demonstrate to a reasonable tenant that he owes this protection to all other tenants. If he will not agree, he is making the rules and you do not want him.

The heat clause is one that will be of concern only where you give heat, of course, and is so worded. You may strike it out but it automatically applies only in those cases where you customarily supply heat. I have always found that it is best to follow the advice of an oldtimer who said, "What's a few gallons of oil or shovels of coal, compared to the profit we make? Give them good heat and keep them satisfied if they are reasonable."

You will invariably find that the heating system of any given building is adequate to keep the building properly warm in zero weather. Often the building is not satisfactorily heated simply because it has gotten out of adjustment or repair. In some cases a radiator or two are plugged or improperly vented. A system that was adequate to heat a building when it was new may not be capable of doing so when the windows have become loose and leaky, allowing a portion of the heat to escape, and causing serious discomfort, not to mention expense.

We should bear in mind that if we want others to live up to our deals, we should be equally willing to do so. The tenant of a heated apartment has no means of keeping warm except through the heat we supply. He cannot be expected to shiver uncomplainingly any more than you or I would.

By accepting him as tenant in a heated apartment, we have undertaken the obligation to furnish reasonable heat. In practically every state this means 70 to 72 degrees, from 7 A.M. to

11 P.M. Fortunately the degree of heat is a measurable thing. And thermometers are very inexpensive.

If the system is defective, have it put in proper condition. Not only will you have satisfied, long term tenants, but you will save fuel. Nothing convinces a tenant that it's time to move more than being cold in the winter.

There is no economy in procrastinating a heat repair. You will want to rent the apartment to another tenant if this one moves out. The new tenant will be no more likely to endure the cold than the old one. So it will have to be straightened out anyway. It is simple common sense to do it early and well. Give the tenant all the heat that is fair, and even be a little generous, allowing for human variants in this regard. And do it with a good heart. It pays.

The unjustified complaint is not difficult to pinpoint. Nor is it arguable when you show a thermometer registering 72 degrees to a tenant. The apartment *is* or *is not* being heated properly. If the thermometer shows 72 degrees it is. A bothersome tenant who insists that he is cold and asks you to touch the cold radiator must be told the facts of life, shown the thermometer, and the conversation should end there. But be right first, and if you are not, accept the responsibility gracefully and do your part.

The case of Mr. P. contained a combination of object lessons. You will remember that I rented the flat to his wife and never had the Vital Interview with him present. After he got out of the service and entered into civilian life, his wife's life became a hell, and Mr. P. tried his best to make mine the same. As soon as I saw that this was another mistake resulting from lack of a proper Vital Interview, I tackled the business of getting rid of him, which was not easy in those days of OPA. Fortunately, he and Mrs. P. separated and she went back to her mother. That left the apartment vacant. I breathed a sigh of relief and rented it to another tenant.

Soon after, the P's reconciled and occupied various places as they separated and tried again, until one day they took the fourth floor apartment in a building owned by one Mr. McG.

Mr. McG. was an interesting chap. He was a simple, direct, honest fellow, almost illiterate, and had been a janitor of several buildings when the depression struck. The owners had abandoned the properties to the banks and, as often happened, the banks had turned over management to the janitor.

When Mr. McG. showed by his actions that he was honest, they urged him to take over as owner, and he did. Thereafter, he ran them in a direct, uncomplicated way. He never bothered with things like applications, credit reports and all that. If you looked OK and wanted the flat, you paid the rent, got a receipt and the key and you moved in. When you wanted to go, you did.

Soon after Mr. P. moved in, Mr. McG's headaches started. Mr. P. had a right to heat, dang it, and he was going to get it. And he was going to get every iota that he was legally and technically entitled to—or else. When Mr. P. found one bedroom (which he didn't use, by the way) that was 67 degrees, he called in the city health authorities as witnesses, and filed complaint in the Brookline Municipal Court against Mr. McG.

Mr. McG. brought me the summons and explained that he was worried. This was the second such complaint by Mr. P. against him and he engaged me for the defense. I was somewhat in a quandary. If I tried to break down the witness, the city inspector, what would he do to me in the apartments *I* owned?

This was the solution we decided upon. I had Mr. McG. install a controlling thermostat in Mr. P's apartment, in the coldest room. Then we went to court and I explained how Mr. McG. was trying his earnest best to make things right, and the case was dismissed. But a bad tenant is just that. The defeat, if such it was, rankled in Mr. P's breast.

All was quiet for a time. Then Mr. McG. started to get his oil bills. He got hold of the repair man quickly and they surveyed the building for the cause of the enormous bills. They noted that the first, second, and third floor tenants kept their windows open in bitter cold weather, and many paraded around their apartments in undershirts, a la July.

Examination of the system showed nothing out of order. But when it came time to check the thermostat, they could not get into Mr. P's apartment. He had changed the lock. He knew his rights. So they had to wait for Mr. P's boy to come home from school and open the door. Of course when they entered, they found that Mr. P. left the beds "to air," and the windows wide open. The thermostat was set at 85. They removed it and installed one that was locked at 72. They closed the windows and left a stern request with the boy about open windows.

This part of the unhappy experience proved the necessity of the application-and-investigation-first technique, and the value of the Vital Interview. But Mr. P. was not yet through with Mr. McG.

A few days later Mr. McG. brought me another summons with which he had been served. This time, on the complaint of Mr. P., he was to answer to a criminal charge of Breaking and Entering, like a burglar. He asked me, "Can he do that to me?" I reiterated my advice that he adopt my methods of handling applicants for apartments. He never adopted them. Nevertheless, by and large, he did well and became very wealthy.

It was routine for the charge to be dismissed, of course. But here was a dramatic example of the protection that our Key Clause affords. If Mr. McG. had had Mr. P. sign such a lease as ours, he could have checked on Mr. P's use of the thermostat periodically, and have been spared a month's abuse of the system.

Besides, the other tenants had now become used to 90 degree heat and it is not easy to accustom yourself to 72 thereafter. You feel as if you are freezing. The whole unhappy thing should have, and easily could have, been avoided.

23

HOW TO HOLD THE PROPERTY

Upon taking title to the property, you will have
open to you a variety of ways in which you may hold it. Some
times the suggestion will be made that you form a corporation
or trust.

The corporate status has many advantages and disadvantages. The prime advantage is the freedom from personal liability and responsibility that you enjoy. But this is limited to
lawsuits on claims such as people tripping on defective stairways. In these cases you are personally free from danger of being sued, since the corporation is the legal owner, not you. You
are a stockholder and officeholder of the corporation. But
there is no real advantage in this so-called protection. Your
insurance will cover these claims and you will be safe in this
regard anyway.

If you were a person who stood in fear of being sued for
other business debts, you might have some advantage in owning
the real estate through a corporation, but this is, from a practical standpoint, the only possible benefit. It is true that the
property of the corporation cannot generally be reached to
apply to the debts of the individual, even where he controls
the corporation.

On the other hand, some folks have tried to acquire real
estate by taking title in the name of a newly formed corpora-

tion for the reverse reason. A buyer knows that whoever takes title must sign the mortgage and mortgage note. Hence, he forms a corporation, and sets things up through his lawyer so that the Corporation, not he individually, becomes the buyer. He will be surprised when the bank insists that it will not give the loan unless the buyer, personally, signs the note as co-maker with the corporation. Thus the sought-after result is not obtained.

From a tax angle, the Corporation has other important disadvantages. Many exemptions afforded the individual owner are not extended to corporations. In many states, as in Massachusetts, the individual who owns real estate is completely free of all STATE income tax on rental income. Even were he to receive a million dollars per month in rental income, it is deemed that the city real estate tax has already taken its bite out of that income, and he does not pay any *state* income tax on it! By the way, I know of one owner whose holdings grew largely through acquiring Aunt Tobys, and whose monthly rental income IS over a million a month! And most of it to this day is from Aunt Tobys. He started without a dime.

From the federal tax angle there are basic taxes that can usually be avoided by 'draining off' the income of the corporation in salaries to the officers so that there is no real disadvantage there. However, you will find that the extra bookkeeping, filing of periodic forms such as Certificate of Condition, State and Federal withholding and other musts, will add bother and responsibility where none need exist.

With very rare exceptions, I do not recommend that you incorporate. Nor is the trust status of any real benefit for the same reasons generally. The benefits of the recommended method of holding title are simpler, less tax finagling is required, and many profitable exemptions will be yours.

There are many varieties of the type of holding that is recommended. In many states it is called Ownership by the Entirety. Others call it Joint Ownership. The effects are virtually the same. The property is deeded by the seller to: John Buyer and Amy Buyer, husband and wife, as Tenants by the Entirety, Or to Henry Buyer and Amy Buyer as Joint Tenants (or in Joint Ownership).

Your lawyer will inform you of the wording used in your state when you tell him what you wish to accomplish. When you and your wife (or husband) own in this manner you are in the best position, tax-wise, that is possible. No advantage has been lost, except in the rare case where a husband is at odds with his wife and wants to be able to resell the property without requiring her signature. For these cases, your lawyer will recommend a special holding method, legal in your state. But for the run-of-the-mill cases, the so-called partnership with the wife is best.

Should either you or your wife die, there will be important inheritance tax benefits, state and federal. Within certain limits, the surviving spouse may claim that there has been no legal inheritance because the property was owned by the entirety. That is, the widow "owned the *entire* property" with her title waiting to be fully cleared by her husband's death. The reverse is also true, of course. Should the wife die, the husband "owned the *entire* estate" before her death anyway.

In so-called Dower Rights States, that is, where the law automatically endows the wife with dower rights in any real estate owned by the husband (whether acquired before or during marriage) the husband cannot sell nor mortgage his property without his wife's signature anyway. So he gives up no important freedom by taking title by the entirety.

24

TAX BENEFITS WHILE HOLDING

In the previous chapter, the state exemption from income tax of all rental income has been mentioned. There are certain other advantages enjoyed by real estate owners which have been said to be the major reason for the truth of the saying "The only way left to get rich in the United States is in real estate."

The tax benefits that we enjoy while we hold the property are usually so profitable that it is easy to see why the saying came into being. To understand the most important one, we should first note that there are few, if any, ways in which a person engaged in business can lawfully receive money in hand that is truly profit, without paying a fat tax on it. But in real estate this is made possible and legal through the medium of depreciation.

It is impossible to over-emphasize the importance of this in your future fortunes. Next only to the fact that the Aunt Toby type of property supplies an essential of life at a unique profit to the supplier, the depreciation item is the greatest single contributor to our getting rich in real estate.

A simple definition of depreciation, as it applies to us, has been offered thus: Depreciation is allowed as a loss on the income tax return of a real estate owner, on the premise that his building has aged and depreciated during the tax year.

Any losses that other taxpayers claim must be actual cash

paid out of hand. Not so for real estate owners. Here a tax "freak" obtains. It amounts to this. Nowhere in this book will you read any other single point that will affect your fortunes more.

Because of a "paper" loss, the cash you receive in hand from tenants is largely exempt from taxation.

The effect of this single phenomenon is far-reaching. Through it we are permitted to keep a substantial part of our income that in any other business would go to the government. In turn, this permits us to *re-invest*. That is, we proceed to invest that money in another and still another building to bring additional profit and additional depreciation allowances. This pyramiding is the *rule*, not the *exception* for real estate investors.

Let us examine, by a simple example, how the depreciation item works.

You buy an Aunt Toby for $22,000. You value the land (and it's largely up to you) at $2,000 and the building at $20,000. Here is how your net taxable income would be affected in the Profit and Loss statement of the building.

Total rents received $4500.00

Less Expenses:

Taxes	$ 800.00
Interest on Mortgages	1160.00
Water	100.00
Insurance	80.00
Repairs	460.00
Depreciation: 5% of $20,000. (3% on brick buildings)	1000.00

Total Expenses & Losses $3600.00

Deduct from income 3600.00

Net taxable profit .... $ 900.00

(But note that the Depreciation item of $1000 is money you actually have NOT paid out!)

Thus, assuming you had no vacancies, you would transfer $900 to your tax return for your regular exemptions and deductions. This is quite different from being forced to pay tax on $1900. Yet you are permitted to receive and use that $1000 for re-investment.

Any tax accountant will tell you that this is a "dream" deal from the tax approach. To be allowed to make a profit of $1900 and actually *receive* $1900 in hand—and to be permitted to pocket $1000 of it tax free (for 20 years) gives you an enormous boost toward becoming wealthy. It is precisely this point that has been the basic reason why real estate owners have received such a huge percentage of their investment back in hand with which they could re-invest, pyramid and *do it quickly!*

Granted that they would have generally received their investment in hand in two, three or four years anyway, we must not overlook the grim truism that anyone who receives profit must not count his blessings until he has lopped off the part that must go to Uncle Sam. It is the allowance for *depreciation* that makes all the difference.

There are other significant tax allowances in the ownership of real estate. You should take full advantage of them. For instance any improvements you make in the building are distinguished from normal repairs. Routine maintenance and repairs are classified as a direct expense and are deductible in full on that year's return.

However, improvements, such as the installation of a new roof or heater are not considered repairs, but are classified as Capital Improvements. From a tax standpoint, you are permitted to take deductions for these, but only over a period of years, usually eight or ten. Thus a $1000 expenditure for a roof permits you to deduct a loss of $100 each year for ten years.

Recently a new law was passed that gave an extra tax exemption to new owners of property. You will want to take advantage of it. Formerly, when you bought a building and spent some substantial sums on improvements, you were limited to taking, as a deduction, 1/8 or 1/10 of the expenditure each year for 8 or 10 years until you had used it up. This still obtains as to roofs, sidewalls, heating systems etc. Some recent changes and clarifications in the tax law have given special benefits to owners who install equipment such as stoves, refrigerators, sinks, airconditioners etc. On these, you can deduct the usual 10% or 12½% *plus* an additional 20% in the first year. (This has a $2000 maximum on the 20% to any one person.)

Let us say you buy a building and install $3,000 worth of equipment. You take the usual $300 (10%) the first year as a deduction, *plus* an additional $600 (20% of $3,000) and your total deduction for the first year is $900 on your tax return.

You will, of course, use up the 100% of the expenditure more rapidly, but it's worth it to get back your investment as soon as possible for re-investment.

Remember, *all* painting is deemed a repair, even though the work is effective as an improvement for many years. You deduct the entire cost of a paint job, exterior or interior *in full* on your next tax return.

25

HOW TO SELL THEM

For some owners, there can be no sweeter, happier life in business than the ownership of the Aunt Tobys, with the comparatively minor attention required. For them ownership and operation of the properties is "nirvana." They are able to live a secure life with uninterrupted income and little bother. Seasoned with just enough responsibility to give meaning to life, as distinguished from complete idleness, they can work or loaf at will. They are not tied down, particularly if they own unheated property. They can go away in summer or winter with carefree heart, leaving only someone to receive and deposit rents and process occasional complaints.

Most owners in this category have another full time occupation and they run their buildings "with the left hand." Management takes so little time or attention that it does not interfere with their work or leisure. Except for a few days in early July, at renting time, you will be able to manage an income of $2000 to $4000 per month by devoting to it less than three hours per month. And even at renting time, you need only give a few evenings to showing and interviewing.

The nearer your property is to a genuine Aunt Toby, the less time you will need to devote and the more freedom from attention and management you will enjoy. At the peak of my ownership, when I had 146 units, I rarely spent more than five hours per month in all, in management, processing incoming rents, complaints and checking on repairs. There is no business in the world, short of a huge investment in income-producing stocks, that can match it.

If you acquire your portfolio of properties you may be one of those who choose to stop there and just enjoy your new life. Some of my graduates have reached this point, and after a time, consulted me as to what I had done as a *step upward* from this pleasant state. When you have reached this point you, too, may want to make that step.

Up to 1955 I busily accumulated the buildings, with no thought of selling anything. It was by sheer accident that the idea of selling came into the picture.

I had just bought No. 16 for $25,000. Soon after signing up, I took a friend, Ken, with me to tour the building. He had made some fine profits on real estate investments through my counsel, but had got cold feet on one that I felt he should have held on to. We called it Griggs Road. The rents were high and his Scotch instincts were much in evidence when there was a vacancy, however short. When he was offered a fat profit for Griggs Road, he came to see me. I said no. The $5,000 or so he would make did not compare with the steady income the property afforded him over the years. But, after some lame rationalization, he decided to sell for $40,000. The same property sold for $60,000 within a few years.

As Ken and I went through No. 16, he fell in love with it. Pressed for a price I quoted $30,000. He replied, "You'll never get $30,000 for that old building. I'll give you $27,000."

I retorted, "I won't get $30,000, eh? Watch me! I'll get $35,000!"

So I sat down to figure out a package. I remembered the experience I had had in unloading the badly located properties and felt that the same technique would work now. A low down payment and a comparatively huge MIF to the buyer were to be the attraction.

I advertised and in a few weeks I had waded through a

dozen who wanted to steal it. But soon I got a customer who
was mainly interested in just two things: "How much do I put
in? How much do I take out each year—*net*—money in my fist!"
He didn't care whom he paid what. He wasn't interested in
what he paid the sums out for. He cared less *how long* the
mortgage was. The rate of interest only mildly concerned him.
The way I had framed the package made it, for such a buyer,
irresistible. He would put in $2800 in cash and his MIF would
figure thus:

Present total rental income	$7,000.00

Payouts:

Taxes	$ 807.00
Fuel	715.00
Janitor	180.00
Elec., other utilities	71.00
Insurance	74.00
Water	88.00
Mortgage to *R. Kent,* $32,200 at 4½% for 22 years, $192.37 per month. Per year	$2,308.44
Total payouts	4,243.44
Leaving the buyer Net Clear in Hand (MIF) per year	$2,756.56

I sent Mr. J. to look the property over. When he came back to
my office we went over the figures. Here is substantially the
way I presented the package. You will want to know how to
prepare and present such a package if you plan to make the
final step upward too. So it is given in the form you will use.

I gave him a pad and pencil and together we made the MIF
sheet as it is above. Now I spelled out for him the figures as
he would live with them:

"These four-room heated apartments are renting now for
about $40 each. The rents are controlled as long as the present
tenants remain. If one moves out or if controls go off altogether,
you increase the rents substantially, *without* increasing your
payouts one cent.

But let's be pessimistic and suppose they do *not* become decontrolled. Here is your package:

You invest	$2,800.
You take in each year	7,000.
You pay out, not including vacancies and repairs, say	4,250.
leaving you in hand	$2,750 per year

This is practically 100% per year on your investment. True, you might have a repair, but, just as likely, you will have a vacancy and that will increase your net—permanently. And that's not all.

Besides making about 100 per cent on your investment, you make about 50 per cent per year *more*. That is, under the above plan, you will be paying off principal on the mortgage, *buying the building*, to the average amount of $1,450 per year.

Now let us consider what happens if rent controls go off. (We expected them to be discontinued within a year, and they were.) You will be able to raise the rents to a reasonable level commensurate with what this type of apartment pays elsewhere. An average of $20 per apartment is very fair. That will give you $2,640 per year additional income without one extra penny of cost to you. That makes another 95 per cent per year on your investment!"

It is not to be wondered at that Mr. J. bought the property that afternoon. He is still happy with it. His MIF is even better than we anticipated.

At this point, you may be asking what became of my mortgage to the bank for the original $19,000? And why did I sell such a gold mine?

Mr. J's lawyer asked about the old mortgage. The plan I worked out for selling the property with the old mortgage still continuing will be your key to making the step upward.

"Your client, Mr. J.," I explained, "will pay mortgage payments only to me. He will pay $192.37 per month for 22 years. Mr. J. is not concerned with the old mortgage. The new one to me will appear as a second mortgage on record since the bank's first mortgage precedes it. But I alone will take care of the old mortgage payments and Mr. J. will not have any connection with it. He just sends me the payments on the new $32,200 mortgage."

Mr. J's lawyer replied, "Suppose you die? Or go broke? What then? My client would have to pay the old mortgage to keep the bank from foreclosing and wiping him out."

To which I had the answer. "Your client will be fully protected. I will give you a signed contract, agreeing that if I should not make the payments on the old $19,000 mortgage to the bank, Mr. J. may *discontinue* payments to me on the new mortgage and send his payment to cover the bank payments. The bank payments are smaller by far than the payments to me on the $32,200 will be. So Mr. J. is fully protected."

After carefully scrutinizing all the aspects of this deal, the like of which he had never before encountered (and neither had I until I evolved it), the lawyer assured Mr. J. that he was perfectly safe. He would never have to pay any obligation on the building greater than the $32,200 mortgage.

So I drew the contract and it was approved. The sale went through as planned and the payments have been coming in to me regularly from Mr. J. Having seen the plan as it appeared from Mr. J's angle, let us examine how I made out.

I originally invested		$6,000.
I made during the 6 months I held it (for tax purposes described soon)	$1500.	
I received down payment from Mr. J.	2800.	
At the time I sold it I had taken back		4,300.
so my net investment after the sale was		$1,700.

The income and outgo figures that I would live with for some 19 years and six months, while I still paid the old mortgage were:

I received each year, payments from Mr. J.	$2,308.44
I send the bank for 19½ years, per year	1,442.42
leaving me net in hand each year	$ 866.02
totalling for the first 19½ years $16,454.38	

In addition to the above, I would have the last 2½ years of payments to me from Mr. J. clear, totalling $5,771.10, or thus I would clear for my $1700, $22,225.48.

When I thus sold the property I had absolutely no bother with it. I was in the position that the bank usually holds, that of mortgagee. The payments had to reach me each month and I would note them in the book. Mr. J. was deliriously happy. He was making a fine profit and the future promised even better return on his money.

When the smoke had cleared, I settled back to contemplate what I had done. Owning the property was certainly sweet, but getting payments every month without even the small bother of ownership was even more attractive. Each month as the payments came in, my investment became safer and safer as the balance on the mortgage was reduced.

It was quite natural that I began to scribble some figures. What would Freeman do for me? I tried it at $40,000. It made a very attractive package—too attractive. So I tried $50,000. Still too much left in hand for the owner. Then I tested the figures as they would work out if I sold for $60,000 with 10 per cent down and a mortgage to me of $54,000 at 20 years. The net in hand to the buyer after payments on that mortgage was a little too small. So I tried it on a basis of a 22 year mortgage which required smaller payments. That was just right. It was a matter of simple figures that took but a few minutes. When I was ready to advertise and present the package here is the MIF as I offered it:

Price: $60,000.

You will pay cash		$6,000.00
Total yearly rents (in 1955)	$7,750.	
Payouts:		
Taxes	$ 933.00	
Insurance	113.00	
Water	60.00	
Mortgage of 4½% for 22 years, $54,000. $322.60 per month or per year	3,871.20	
Total payouts		4,977.20
leaving you net in hand (MIF)		$2,772.80

In a few weeks I had sold Freeman to Mr. N. Even after normal repairs he would clear over 50 per cent per year on his investment, MIF. Besides, as in the case of Mr. J., he would have the tenants paying off the mortgage for him, in effect buying the property for him, at an average rate of about $2,454 per year. And all this was on the *pessimistic* prediction that rent controls would *not* go off. But we all felt certain they soon would, as they did. When this happened Mr. N's MIF increased some 50 per cent without unfairness to the tenants, and he has never missed a payment to me. We would clear some $115,000 in payments on this deal and my family and I were free of care and responsibility.

I now bought the biggest car on the American market to accommodate my three tall sons and all our luggage. We put the car on the USS *United States* and set out to tour Europe again. In my wallet I carried a slip with some figures. They showed what Freeman and No. 16 had provided for us. It was my intention to meditate and decide whether to sell more properties, on the same basis, or hold them. It was easy to figure what type of payments each of them would carry and still leave a buyer a very attractive MIF. I now also recognized that the average real estate investor was only dimly aware of, or interested in, the details of his mortgage. It seemed to me, figuratively speaking, that it was easier to get a buyer who would pay $100 per month for 20 years, to be paid in full, than it was to get one who would pay $125 per month for ten years.

When we returned from the trip, I had decided to sell. I planned to write some mortgages for 30 years and others for 22 or 25 years. Not only was I going to sell the properties I owned, but I hoped to buy some here and there as I could and package and sell them, too.

As soon as you have become known in the community as a buyer of Aunt Tobys you will find more and more of them being offered to you. You will have a distinct and decisive advantage in these deals. You *can* wait. The seller cannot wait or doesn't want to. Several times I have bought property at the first price

I named, with the offer being snapped up so quickly that it led me to inquire later as to the reason.

When I offered Mr. BH a flat figure for his building, he grabbed it, only specifying that my offer must be firm. If the offer was to contain a reservation that only if I could obtain certain financing was I obligated to go through with the deal, he would not sign. At the time I had finances available if the bank failed me, so I signed him up. Then I asked him about it.

"It's this way," said BH, "I have put a deposit of $1,000 on a new house in Hamilton. I *must* come up with the balance on the first of October, or lose my deposit. Here it is September and I've been trying to sell for months. I had decided that the next tenable offer which guaranteed that I would have the cash before October 1, would be accepted. I have no other way of paying for the house I signed for."

In another deal, a widow had placed her Aunt Toby with me for sale as broker. After she moved out of the state, she received reports from me periodically as to my efforts to sell. I forwarded all offers. One day she phoned me long distance.

"What can you get for the house right away?"

I urged patience. Real estate can never be sold quickly, no matter how attractive, with the possible exception of a single house in a most-wanted area, at a very low price, and in the selling season.

She pressed for an answer. "What can we sell it for?"

I told her that I could conduct an auction or put it on the market for a slashed price but she would probably realize only $12,000 after my commission was deducted.

"OK, sell it!" she snapped.

"If you really want to get rid of it that strongly—" I began and she cut in with, "I want it off my hands. I'm sick of it. I want an end to the thing."

I asked, "Would you want to sell it to me, personally, at $12,000 net?"

"It makes no difference to me," she replied. So I bought it, for cash.

Six months * and a few days later I sold it for $22,500. I arranged a very attractive package and a local grocer is living there now, rent free, and very happily. He will pay us for 25 years.

Time on your side is a most powerful factor in almost every business. You do not have any great pressure to buy, but often your seller is under any one of many pressures to sell quickly.

And once you have bought, having first checked that you will be making a fine profit during the time you hold the property, you are in no hurry to sell. The selfsame facts and figures that made you buy the property will be on your side when you wish to sell. In general you will be selling to a workingman who is fed up with paying rent and wants to start accumulating something besides rent receipts. The majority of your buyers will be men who work at some mechanical trade. They do not fear the expense of small repairs like the man who cannot handle a screwdriver. Most of the mechanics have many spare hours which they plan to put to use improving their houses. This, of course, improves your security on the mortgage you hold, on the property, and everyone benefits.

The examples above demonstrate the motives that impel an investor to buy larger parcels. There is little difference in preparing a package that will be irresistible to the buyer of a three-family Aunt Toby. The only variation is that your package will spell out that he will have *his apartment free, plus* so much a month MIF. In some cases, you will have an MIF that shows that the buyer will have to pay some nominal amount out of pocket each month, on top of the rents, to cover all payments. This is more often the case where heat is supplied.

But you have the additional inducement of the principal payments that he is "pocketing each month" to make the package still more attractive. If, for instance, there is going to be a mortgage to you for $14,000, for 20 years, you can honestly show that he will be gaining an average of $700 per year in paying off the building. The long-range outlook for a secure retirement with no mortgage to pay after the 20 years is a tempting vision. That's when he wants it most.

So you can show that he will be doing fine during the years

he is (or rather the tenants are) paying off the mortgage, and doing even better, much better, after the mortgage is paid. To establish how many years you want your mortgage to run, you should take into consideration your age. It is well known that men live longer if secure. So tack about 10 years on to your general life expectancy as the insurance companies calculate it, and fix your mortgage periods accordingly. Some consideration should be given to Social Security payments you will receive after you have reached the required age. Since owning real estate or mortgages is not classified as holding a job, you will suffer no deductions because of your income.

If your prospective buyer is income-tax minded, you will point out the fact that if he is in the 30% bracket, the government is, in effect, paying 30% of his Real Estate taxes, the mortgage interest, the fuel bill and the repair bills. You can explain the depreciation item, too.

To demonstrate just how you fared on a typical Aunt Toby that you bought, held a while, and sold, we will follow it through.

When you bought it, you paid $11,500. You put $1500 down and assumed a mortgage of $10,000 at 6% for 20 years. In order to get the benefit of long term capital gain, you must keep the property at least six months. Let us say you keep it five years. You put it on the market, advertising as your head line

"Your rent $00.00 per month."

(*or*)

"YOUR APT. RENT-FREE PLUS $19 per month clear. Buy this handsome 3-family, with separate heaters with only $900 down..."

As a general rule, you made some profit while you held the building. Your present investment is now $00. Now you offer a buyer this package:

Price	$15,000.
Down payment	900.
Your income—from 2nd and 3rd floor apartments	$ 150. per month

You pay out:

Taxes .... $30 per month.

Mortgage interest and
principal on $14,100
at 6% for 25 years—
per month 90.86

Water, insurance, etc. 10.
_____

Total payouts .... $130.86 per month
deducted from income of $150 per month,
leaves you *your apartment rent free and*— $19.14 per mo. in hand

Of course, you can make the mortgage 20 years and have
more in hand clear for yourself, and you do not get nearly as
much out of the deal as if you managed the property and cared
for it, but when you have enough of them paying you, the net in
hand becomes very substantial and secure.

In making this presentation to a prospective buyer you will
usually have paid the old mortgage down substantially by the
time you sell the property. But even if you just buy them, keep
them six months * or more and sell them, each one establishes a
life income that is very pleasant.

In making these presentations to prospective customers, you
should be very specific. Arrange a "package" which leaves no
room for guesswork.

The lesson in package arrangement was driven home to me
by my experience in buying and selling a little duplex in Cam-
bridge. I had bought the property early in the spring of one
year and had been advertising it for some six months before I
suddenly realized that immediate and drastic measures were
indicated.

During those six months * I was deeply involved in the big
Collonades property and paid little attention to the duplex
other than answering calls and occasionally running over to
meet a prospect and show the house. When Collonades was all
sewed up, it was fall and time to worry about freezing pipes
in unoccupied buildings. I reviewed the entire duplex transaction to this point and tried to put my finger on the reason it
did not sell

I had paid some $2700 for it. When I started advertising it I priced it at $5900. When a few months passed without a buyer, I lowered the price to $4900. Then a few months later to $3900. Still no buyer. As I reviewed it, I was more than ever convinced that it was a good honest buy for the right party, if I could but find that party, *and present the proposition correctly.*

The ads that I had been running were terse and clear, but they did not take into consideration the attitudes and experience of the customer I was appealing to. This property could only appeal to a working man of humble status. If you stop to think a moment it is apparent that this working man had read many ads before. The furniture that was advertised at $25 down and $28 per month turned out to cost him $100 down and $50 per month. The car he saw advertised to cost $99 down and $22.68 per month turned out, after the salesman salved and switched him, to be $270 down and $51 per month, et cetera. It is not surprising then that he was hardened to taking ads with a large grain of salt. It seemed to me that the way to overcome this distrust was to meet it head on, with the kind of directness and unmistakable truthfulness that would make him feel that this ad meant precisely what it said, and that he would not meet the standard "borax" or bait advertising technique if he came to look at my property. So I framed an ad and ran it in the *Boston Globe.* Here it is:

CAN YOU PAY $900 DOWN?
CAN YOU PAY $19.50 PER MONTH?

This well-built duplex will cost you *exactly* that much. You live in one side and collect the rent from the other side, *add exactly* $19.50 from your pocket, send it to the bank, and *that's all.* (There are NO extras!) You have paid INTEREST, PRINCIPAL AND TAXES. Price Only $3900. Each side of the duplex has 5 rooms, separate heat, large kitchen and a nice yard. I will be there from 10 to 12 today. Come over and bring your deposit.

Robert W. Kent, 310 Harvard St., Brookline. 734-3211.

When I arrived at the building at ten o'clock, a man was waiting for me. He later told me that his wife had been watching the ads for years, waiting for someone to tell her in clear and unequivocal terms the exact and *truthful* amount that would be required as down payment and monthly payments. When she saw this ad, she handed him $200 and told him to go and see it, and if he was pleased with the house and if the ad "said the truth," buy it.

Within the hour I could have sold a dozen. People begged me to give them at least the "second chance" to buy it if the present buyer backed out. Finally I hung a card in the window saying, "Property sold. Thanks for coming," and left. This little deal was probably the outstanding error of my real estate career.

When I sat down to analyze what I had done, the error struck me. This customer had not even *asked* how long his mortgage would run! And to this day I do not think he cared. His ONLY concern was with two questions:

How much down? (and that meant *really* how much.)

How much a month? (again—the truth.)

It was apparent that he didn't really care how much the house cost! Even the price was relatively unimportant.

Actually I was taking back a fifteen year mortgage, but it would not have mattered one whit if I had taken one for 25 years—at the same monthly payments. My entire approach to the problem of selling had been wrong in the earlier efforts. I had lowered the price repeatedly, thinking to thus make the deal attractive. That was not where the trouble lay. I had cut my profit in the deal some 75 per cent in this effort, and it had been entirely unnecessary. I had thrown away $3000.

From that day on I have practiced and taught the lesson that this deal taught me. Our presentation must be made with one dominating rule obtaining throughout. We must *think* and *read* with the eyes of the man who will read the ads. We must never forget that in practically every instance, he has never bought a house before. He fears that which he does not understand. He fears that there are a thousand gimmicks whereby he will be charged for things that he does not understand nor anticipate, and that he will be burdened with an obligation that he will not be able to carry. Further, we should remember that this buy is the biggest single purchase the buyer has made in his lifetime. This alone is enough to fill him with terror. Unlike the duplex buyer, the period of payments also may add to his terror. Our customer well remembers signing up for the car, or refrigerator. That was three years, and seemed a lifetime. The payments on a house will be on his shoulders for *twenty* years! If we are to be successful in presenting our package, we must realize that these fears and terrors exist in the minds of our prospective buyers.

Our package must say to him, *in his language,* "You need not fear. Nobody will even *try* to raise the figures of down payment and monthly payments. There *are* no extras that will be sprung on you. The fact that you have never bought a house before need cause you no concern. This deal holds no tack-on's, no extras. Nor will a salesman use this ad to lure you into his clutches and then sell you something far less attractive, or more expensive. You have nothing to fear. If you can make the advertised down payment and the advertised monthly payments, you can buy this property with a free heart."

It may be inaccurate to say that the mistake I made in the duplex deal was entirely a loss. Some time later I collected a fat fee for a consultation on a problem. I needed only the experience of the duplex to solve it. The analysis of the problem and its solution will help you in selling.

When I sat down with my client to consult, he had asked his assistants to sit in on the conference, and help. The problem, as presented to me, was this: The client owned some 19 houses in a not-to-desirable city north of Boston. The city had suffered when manufacturers deserted it for southern locations. Now the population depended on a large plant that was mostly engaged in government work. The client, Mr. P., had owned the buildings for over two years and had tried about everything to move them. He had lowered prices, of course, and that reminded me of the duplex experience. That hadn't helped. He had stepped up his advertising without result, too. The buildings represented a loss each month they were held vacant, and had been held so long that he had given up making any profit.

It was unnecessary to inquire into the honesty and truthfulness of the packages that the client had been offering. The client was a square dealer. My next inquiry was a careful dissection of the deals to see whether they were understandable and whether the buyer was being offered fair value. It is pointless to try to find a way to sell a dollar's worth for $2. The properties matched their prices fairly.

Next I examined a few sample ads that had been used to find buyers. They were written by Mr. P. himself. He knew all about real estate. He had forgotten that the buyers did not. The answer started to emerge.

Next I asked some of the staff who had talked with prospects, what the answers and reactions of the prospective customers had been.

The sales manager said, "Well, I remember talking to one fellow who made a great point of asking me repeatedly what OTHER expenses he would have to pay besides the advertised $28.60 per month. Each time I told him that was all he would have to pay he came back with, 'Yeah, but what else do I have to pay?'"

"Okay," I said, "We've got one customer reaction. Let's jot down the *fears* of these prospective buyers. Number one: *fear of bigger payments.* Let's have some more. Those of you who have talked with buyers, what else have they said?"

"I remember a few," said a salesman, "and one in particular asked me about plumbing and other repairs. Said he knew a fellow who had once bought and then got hung with huge repair bills."

"Fine," I replied, "we have number two: *fear of repair bills.*"

Soon the others came up with reactions from their experiences. Number three on the list was: *fear of being stuck with the house and having to stay though unhappy.*

Number four was: *fear that other tenants would pester the new owner with complaints and demands for services and repairs.* By this time the solution was apparent.

When I made my report, it had the effect of shocking the client at first. "Are you serious, Bob?" he demanded. "You're really suggesting that we sell houses on a free trial, money-back-on-request basis? This is real estate—not cans of shoe polish!"

"It's your best way of wiping out fear, Mr. P.," I insisted. "And I am convinced that it is only fear that stands in the way of your selling the houses."

"Precisely how do you propose we do this?" he asked.

"You advertise the properties *using words and expressions that the working man* will feel are clear and dependable. You offer to sell them on this basis:

"You can buy this house on a *free trial basis*. You have nothing to fear, nothing to lose. You deposit $1200 and we give you the deed. You move in and *try it out* for a year. You own it. You collect rents, make your payments. If you are completely satisfied and the house is just what you want, you go along. About the time you are ready to retire, you've paid off your building in full and you enjoy complete ownership—income—security.

"If you decide you do not want it, and *you alone* are the judge, you simply bring in the deed, lay it on the desk, and say you want your money back. *That's all.* You don't need any reason. Nobody will argue with you. We will take out $40 per month for rent for the months you occupied and refund the rest of your down payment, and thank you.

"This is your opportunity to own your home and income with *no risk*. You have everything to gain and not one cent to lose."

That will be the pattern and spirit of all ads. A few taped radio talks by the owner in person, to present the package, with emphasis on the fact that the buyer who wants a refund does not need any reason for his decision, will help, too.

When a salesman meets some of the customers' fears, he has a solution that will serve to completely reassure the buyer. For instance, if the buyer is afraid to buy because there may be big repair bills, the free trial is the answer. Surely the buyer will find out, within one year, whether the building does need any

repairs. If he finds that there are more repairs needed than he
anticipated, he *is not stuck* with them. He can return the deed↖
and he is out of the deal, completely.

If the buyer is hesitating because he wonders whether this
deal is like the unhappy experience he previously signed for,
wherein he answered an ad that said $25 a month, only to learn
later that he was hooked for much more—this must overcome
that fear. Within a year he will surely determine what the
true carrying cost is. Then if he is not happy, he is not forced
to keep the house. He gets his money back without argument.

And so on with the other fears, whatever they may be. But I
must emphasize this warning: Use words and expressions that
leave no room for doubt and that are in his language—even if
you must resort to the vernacular and slang. Be direct. Be clear.
Be definite in a way that leaves no doubt in the reader's mind.

Every house in the group was sold within three months and
the plan had some pleasant side-effects. Many came to the
office, attracted by the unique plan, inspired by confidence in
a firm which would lean over to be fair, and they bought other
properties without money-back reservations.

The plan is now used whenever a property is too long on
hand. Thus far not one buyer has asked for a refund. Not only
were the packages true, but once the buyer tasted the heady
wine of ownership, he rarely wanted to go back to the lowlier
status of tenant. He liked collecting much better than paying.
He nursed his property. It was a mark of achievement and
status to him. It represented proof of his rise in the world. It
lifted him out of the class of most of his fellow workers. And it
promised to partially support him in his old age.

---

* To get ALL these Capital Gains tax benefits you must now hold the
property at least 1 year AND take depreciation on the straight-line basis. If
you've held it less than 1 year but more than 6 months, you get almost all
that benefit. You can ascertain the precise percentage at your local IRS office.
If you take any kind of *accelerated* depreciation, a whole new set of laws
apply and you get very little capital gains benefits unless you hold the
property 10 years.

26

TAX ANGLES IN SELLING

There are such special and unique benefits and exemptions afforded to real estate operations that it has given rise to this saying:

The tax is never a good reason for *not* selling real estate.

This unique advantage is not given to any other field of investment. To best understand the capital gains benefits afforded exclusively to Real Estate investment, we compare our investment with another—investment in stocks.

Note that in all that follows, we speak only of those investments that you keep for a minimum of six months. These are classified on the Federal Tax level as long-term capital gains, as compared with those we keep for shorter periods. All that I say here applies only to long-term holding of property, and only to Federal Income Tax, not State.

Let us say you buy $10,000 worth of X stock, keep it for seven months, and sell it. In the sale you make a profit of $3,000. Now, says Uncle Sam, you may take one-half of the profit, or capital gain, and put that in your pocket, tax free. The other half, or $1500, you enter in the proper place on your tax return, and pay your regular tax on it.

Now suppose you sold the stock and LOST money instead. Let us assume you sold it for $6,000 for a loss of $4,000. Uncle Sam now allows you to deduct this loss on your tax return but not more than $1000 per year, against your other income. This is limited to 5 years * and, as a result, a maximum total deduction of $5000 no matter how large the loss (unless you have *capital gains* against which to offset the loss). The next does not apply to a "real estate dealer," one who buys and sells real estate primarily for profit. If you are a real estate *operator*, who buys and sells property but only incidentally to your ownership and management of it, there is a special rule which seemingly does not balance out and which is set up for your advantage in a most remarkable way.

Suppose you bought a piece of real estate and held it eight months.* Then you sold it at a profit of $5,000. In this part of the example, the profit is treated precisely as in the case of profit on stocks. You put one-half the profit in your pocket tax free and enter the other half on your return as a long-term capital gain. You must pay your income tax on this one-half. But how big a percentage you pay in tax is limited, upwards, but not downwards.

If your regular tax bracket is, let us say, 30 per cent, you will pay a tax of 30 per cent *of that half*. If it is 40 per cent, you will pay 40 per cent of that half. But if you should be fortunate (?) enough to be in the 70 per cent bracket, the law puts a limit on the tax for your benefit. *In no case* are you required to pay a Federal income tax on *that* half of the capital gain, of more than 50 per cent of *that half*.*

That, of course, amounts to a net of 30–32 per cent tax as a limit on the entire profit on the deal. This is a very low figure, all considered. After all, the percentage of tax at this rate is very close to the lowest bracket on the list.*

Now we come to the most remarkable part. Let us say you LOST $5,000 on the sale of the real estate. If the same policy that obtained in the sale of the stock applied here, you would only be permitted to deduct $1000 per year with a maximum of $5000 total. But *not so in real estate losses!* You enter the *entire* loss on your return, and you are permitted to deduct it all from your year's income. Thus you get the benefit both ways, win or lose. That most vital factor in all investment, income tax, gives that break only to real estate investors. Its effect on your prog-

* Now no limit. You can take it forever until absorbed.

**Now 30–32%

ress toward your million will be a determining element therein.

Besides the capital gains tax advantage previously described here, the outstanding tax benefit we have in selling real estate happens to coincide perfectly with our most advantageous plan for selling. My Certified Public Accountant, Sid Feinberg, has worked this one out with me and guided most of my moves in the tax picture. It is called the Installment Basis of selling and, of course, our best interests are served by selling on that basis.

In simple language, this is what the Installment Basis rule provides: If you sell a piece of real estate, after keeping it at least 6 months * for profit, and you receive *less* than 30 per cent of the sale price in the first year, you are entitled to use the Installment Basis for paying capital gains tax on the profit. The 30 per cent must include all principal payments you receive in that first year, too. It is clear that when you sell something on installments, it is never certain that you are going to be paid in full for it. Hence you pay taxes on that part of the principal payments that you receive *as you receive it*. You do not pay your tax on the entire profit you hope to make, when and if you are paid for the property.

This has a tremendous effect on your method of selling real estate. When you reach the point where you want to start selling your buildings, if, indeed, you ever do decide to do so, you will want to avail yourself of the rule, and certainly you will find that it has a salutary effect on your ability to hold on to the down payment for further investment, instead of having to pay it to the government as tax on the profit on the deal.

It was the Installment Basis rule that permitted me to sell the Collonnades Block. Without it, neither could I have sold it, nor would it have been practical to sell it, even had I been able to find a buyer who could make a large enough down payment.

The Collonnades Block consisted of a long block of brick buildings that ran from corner to corner, on Washington Street, Brookline. There were nine stores, including the post office, and 12 offices and 26 apartments on the second, third and fourth floors. Around the corner on Station Street, was a storage warehouse that formed part of the deal.

I bought the entire parcel for $115,000 in 1947. This was the big deal that occupied my attention while the little duplex deal was distracting it. As soon as I had signed the agreement with the seller, I advertised the warehouse for sale or rent. I had no experience with warehouses and wanted only the front block for my holdings. A few days later an elderly gentleman phoned me and asked if he could sell the warehouse for me. I agreed and quoted $100,000. How he went about it is an amusing little story.

He opened the Yellow Pages of the phone directory to "warehouses" and proceeded to phone each one of them. He would ask, "Do you know anyone who wants to buy a storage warehouse?" Sometimes the party would hang up. Other times he got a polite answer. But he persisted. After he had gone through the A's and B's, and as he worked on the C's he struck pay dirt. This warehouseman was overcrowded and needed more space. The outcome was that I signed up to sell the warehouse for $75,000 to this warehouseman, and arranged to pass papers and the deed simultaneously with my purchase of the entire parcel.

When it came time to consummate the deal, I was hard put to keep the parties apart. Of course, I did not want the seller to know how much I was getting for the warehouse part of the parcel, not that there was much he could do about it then, as he had to go through with it anyway. So I hopped from office to office, signing one thing, delivering another, receiving a deed here, giving one there, until the entire transaction was finished and I heaved a sigh. Now I owned Collonnades at a net cost of $43,750, which included the commission I paid the elderly broker. When I had time to think, I felt stupid for not selling the warehouse myself, but you can't have everything. Soon I placed a new mortgage on it for $58,000.

Now when I was ready to sell Collonnades under the new plan, the thing would have been impossible without the Installment Basis rule.

The package I offered included a price of $185,000 (yes,

that's what I sold it for) and a down payment of $20,000, with a first mortgage to me for $165,000. As usual, I had tested package after package to see how much the income would carry and still leave the buyer a fat return on his investment. When I reached $185,000, I found it to be the virtual limit.

However, I had been taking depreciation during the time I held the building, and in the language of the tax experts, the cost to me at this time was $35,000. I stood to make $150,000. If I were forced to pay even the one-half-of-one-half, that is 25 per cent of the profit as tax, all in one year, the down payment would not cover the tax of $37,500.

But all I received of the purchase price, including the payments in the first year, amounted to less than $23,000. Of this, a little over ⅘ was gain. I was allowed to put half that profit into my pocket, tax free. The other half was subject to my regular tax bracket, but in no case, would I have to pay more than 50 per cent tax *on this half*, even though my tax bracket for the year was greater than 50 per cent.

As the payments come in each month, the part that is principal is recorded in my little book, and the part that is interest in a separate column. One-twelfth of the annual taxes is deposited by each of my buyers with me each month. When the tax bill comes, we square up the balance and I forward the money to the town treasurer. The receipted bills are sent back to the buyers.

The taxes that are deposited with me each month to be turned over to the tax collector in November of each year are not, of course, income. In the following figures, we consider only those sums which are sent me each month as interest and principal. The Collonnades Block

showed as profit during the time I held it	$ 46,000.00
I received down payment from buyer	20,000.00
My wife and I receive payments on a $165,000 mortgage at 4½% for 30 years, $836.07 per mo. ..	300,985.20
Total proceeds from the deal	$336,985.20
less what I put in	43,750.00
Net cleared on the deal	$323,235.20

Note that when I say "my wife and I" receive the income, this is because of a holding plan that you will want to emulate. You will remember that the recommended way in which you and your wife should *hold* title to the property was "as tenants by the entirety," or its equivalent in your state, sometimes known as "joint ownership," etc. It is also permissible for you to hold such assets as mortgages, promissory notes, bank accounts, and stocks in the same way. Thus mortgages are given to *Robert W. Kent and Isabelle R. Kent, husband and wife, as tenants by the entirety*. The accompanying promissory notes are likewise made out to us. The inheritance tax, probate, and other benefits have been described in the chapter on How to Hold the Property.

I have been asked how come the original owner of the Collonnades parcel sold it to me? And for such a price as permitted me to turn such a quick and staggering profit?

There was absolutely nothing that I knew other than what you have learned in this book. The key to it was the method of appraisal that the seller used.

Collonnades had been owned by a former clothier who invested his wealth in income real estate. When he died the estate was turned over to a highly reputable agent for management. The heirs of the clothier spent most of their time on the Riviera, content to receive the monthly checks from the managing agent. In time, they married other wealth and it was decided to liquidate the real estate holdings. The agent calculated the values as he had been accustomed to do. Prices were put on the various pieces. One was offered to me for a price which my Formula indicated was not worth nearly as much. But the price of $115,000 for Collonnades was far below what the Formula said it was worth. Later developments bore this out, as we have seen.

When I sold Collonnades, there was still a mortgage of $58,000 on it. However, my buyer was not responsible for the old mortgage. I alone remained responsible for it and we made a simple contract to that effect. As usual, his attorney was puzzled upon first meeting this arrangement, but after a careful examination, approved. The sale was consummated with a new $165,000 mortgage from the buyer to me, and he has been paying punctually. The policy of giving the buyer a good MIF has paid off. It was necessary to stretch the period of the mortgage to 30 years so that the payments would be small enough to leave the buyer a good MIF. This, however, suited my purposes admirably.

The conclusion is inescapable. Irrespective of the size of the sale, the buyer is far more interested in the *size* of the payments and the resultant MIF than he is in the number of years the mortgage is to run, or the price of the building. I am firmly convinced that the buyer of the Collonnades would not have been interested at $100,000, if the MIF had been small. Incidentally, the buyer of Collonnades is an accountant by profession. If he doesn't understand figures, who does?

One big advantage you will achieve by selling a property occasionally is that you will gradually accumulate larger sums of money which will enable you to use cash as a decisive inducement in your purchases. I respect the ancient adage that "There is no price great enough for a thing that makes a living for you." But as soon as you have found that there are plenty of Aunt Tobys to supply your future needs, you should not be averse to selling one occasionally, if you get your price and terms. It is only if you wish to sell that you need make the terms as attractive as you have learned here to do.

The sales we have described here are largely those in which the buyer was attracted by low down payment and easy terms, with resultant large MIF. You can better those terms if you simply put the property up for sale, arrange a good price, and hold out for it. Your buyer must get his own mortgage, or pay you 25 per cent down, or you simply will not sell. The very fact that you are not in any hurry, that you are making more money every month you hold the parcel, is your best ally. You can wait until you get the deal you want—happily. Your own ambitions and objectives will decide the path you will pursue. If you want to make yourself "well-fixed at forty" as I did, with your first million made, you may choose the livelier, and perhaps riskier path I chose. You may find your situation cozy, secure and delightful when you have acquired a dozen or two Aunt Tobys, and want to stop there. It is understandable. It's a most enviable position in life.

Whichever path you choose, you need only avoid the well-meaning friend who counsels so wisely that you will go broke. Brush him into limbo with the one who declares positively that there are no more opportunities. Make the firm determination that there IS plenty of opportunity for you and that you now know how to use it, and no negative cloud will be permitted to stand in your path to your goal. Roll up your sleeves and go ahead! This is the greatest business in the world!

INDEX

INDEX